MEME
LIFE

The social, cultural, and psychological
aspects of memetic communication

MEME LIFE

The social, cultural, and psychological
aspects of memetic communication

Shane Tilton, Ph.D.

OHIO NORTHERN UNIVERSITY

leyline

Leyline Publishing, Inc.
Fort Worth, TX

First Published in 2022
By Leyline Publishing
1650 West Rosedale Street, Suite 305, Fort Worth, TX 76104

Leyline Publishing, Inc.
1650 West Rosedale Street, Suite 305
Fort Worth, Texas 76104
www.leylinepublishing.com | www.geektherapeutics.com

Printed in the United States of America
10 9 8 7 6 5 4 3 2 1

Library of Congress Cataloging-in-Publication Data is available upon
request.

9781955406000 (trade paper)
9781955406017 (e-book)

Editing and Proofreading by Anthony M. Bean
Copyediting by Madeline Jones
Text Design and composition by Asya Blue Design
Printed by Versa Press
Cover Design by dkmrgn design

ACKNOWLEDGMENTS

This is more than a book.

The words, images, and ideas that comprise the tome that is in front of you represents nearly five years of labor, research, and teaching. These acknowledgments are a poor attempt to thank the vast number of people and organizations that have helped me along the way to complete this project. There will be people that I forget due to my own ignorance. Please accept my apologies for not noting your contributions here.

Brandy Tilton needs to be recognized first for supporting me along the way, including copy-editing my 73,448-word dissertation. I decided to save her that madness by getting others to do that work for this book. She is my biggest cheerleader and the love of my life.

I need the thank my support staff of Nano, Gray Eye, Juniper, Smokey, Minerva, Mambo, Roscoe, and Bitsy, as my cats are always my fiercest critics, especially when I am the only thing standing between them and dinner.

Much love needs to be sent to my grandma (Shirley Schaum) my dad (Jeff), my mom (Debbon), my step-dad (Jim), my step-mom (Becky), my uncles, my aunts, my cousins, my step-sisters, and my step-brothers, as it is fair to say most of them still don't quite understand what I do, yet they still love me.

I would like to thank Dr. Anthony Bean and the rest of the staff of Leyline Publishing. Their input and guidance has made this book better. I am in their debt.

My appreciation also goes to Don Caldwell and the rest of the Know Your Meme staff for their insight and guidance into memetic culture.

The main reason that this book has finally been published after 18 months of consistent writing and rewriting is in part the support I received from all of my colleagues, students, and former students from the Ohio Northern University School of Social Sciences and Human Interaction and the Institute of Civics and Public Policy. I would especially like to thank Erin Swick, Greg Phipps, Jenny Walton, Jeff St. Onge, and Mark Cruea from Communication and Media Studies, Justine Post and Bryan Lutz from Writing and Multimedia Studies, and Dean Holly Baumgartner of the Getty College of Arts and Science at Ohio Northern University for their encouraging words for the past two years.

This book would not exist without the hard work of Tommy Weston Adams III, Elizabeth Cozad-Howard, and Jermaine McGhee. Their writing added the spark needed to complete this book and injected a layer of wisdom that I could not provide.

I also need to thank Dr. Terri Senft from Macquarie University. She is one of the main reasons that I started down the pathway of studying memes and memetic culture. Her kindness, wisdom, and knowledge made me a better researcher and scholar in the process of writing this book.

Ruth A. Deller from Sheffield Hallam University deserves a ton of praise for being my first co-author and allowing me to work with her on an amazing article about how charitable memes gave cultural identity to the United Kingdom. Her thoughtfulness and attention to detail made me a better writer.

I would not be the scholar I am today without the amazing people that served as my graduate school committee members for the decade that I was at Ohio University. My gratitude extends to George Korn, Michael Williams, Michelle Brown, Marc Cutright, Valerie Martin Conley, Stan Alost, and Andrea Baker for being my guides through the long process of earning my doctorate. I also owe a debt that can never be repaid to Duncan Brown, Mia Consalvo, and Eric Rothenbuhler for serving as the chairs of those committees.

This book would not exist if it weren't for the foundational

ACKNOWLEDGMENTS

work done by Limor Shifman and Ryan M. Milner. Their groundbreaking scholarship helped shape my ideas and influenced my
understanding of memes.

It would be impossible to give enough thanks to all my former
students and colleagues at the Ohio University of Zanesville, Ohio
University Lancaster, Muskingum University, and the Instruc-
tional Communication & Research program at the University of
Kentucky's College of Communication and Information. They
made me the higher education professional I am today.

The book would not be in the form it is today without Kortney
Cottle, Holly Dyer, Alexander Dyke, Tim Eilola, Austin Gammell,
Connor Gillmor, Emma M. Green, Ashley Ochsenhirt, Mike Schroeder, Joe Sidoti, Cole Arroyo, Harleigh Bellmann, Johnny Davis,
Mimi Jakes, Evan Kauffman, Bekah Lee, and Eiichi Yokoyama.
Their scholarship advanced my understanding of the topic and
allowed me to be more explicit in my research on the subject. I
hope the following ten chapters are a reflection of those past conversations of the nature of memes.

I need to thank my conference family (Emory & Melissa
Daniel, Anthony & Holiday Bean, Rachel Kowert, Sarah Hays,
Kelli & Jack Dunlap, Rafael Boccamazzo, Ryan Kelly, Lea Hughes,
Adam Jones, Adam Davis, Megan Connell, Jamie Madigan, Ran-
dall Hampton, Jared and Elizabeth Kilmer, Amelia Herbst, Jess
Stone, Steph Orme, Arienne Ferchaud, John Savage, Emily Layne
Floyd, Alex Abrate, Maria Barreras, Adam Hill, Seth Zhai, Daniel
Kaufmann, and Joseph Atanasio) for always breaking me out of
whatever rut I am in at the moment.

Aspects of this book were influenced by the thought-pro-
voking and mind-clearing conversations I've had with Kalhan
Rosenblatt, Taraneh Azar, Matt Schimkowitz, and Earl Hopkins
about the connection between memes and current events. I am in
their debt as well.

forii

I need to thank Jeff and Lori Martin from True Dungeon and Andy and Kristen Looney from Looney Labs for crafting games that were a wonderful distraction in between writing chapters. I also need to thank The Mountain Goats, Andrew Bird, Alexrainbird Music, The Tragically Hip, Eytan Mirsky, Winterpills, Milk Carton Kids, The Main Squeeze, Vulfpeck, Theo Katzman, Gogol Bordello, Chillhop Radio, Dave Matthews Band, and Kerrigan-Lowdermilk for producing great music to listen to while writing.

It also goes without saying that this book was heavily influenced by the work that Mike Rugnetta and the PBS Idea Channel did from their five-year run between 2012 and 2017. Their creative energies found a home in my writing.

Finally, shoutout to California King, Due By Friday, Back to Work, Young Nostalgia, The Geek Bracket, Fun City, The Black Door, Psychology of Video Games Podcast, Note to Self, Busy Philipps is Doing Her Best (with the always amazing Caissie St. Onge), The Horne Section Podcast, Reply All, Small Beans Audio!, The Underculture with James Adomian, and Tundra Talk for being my podcast playlist for the past year.

As always, thank you, Nick.

Shane Tilton
June 15, 2021

TABLE OF CONTENTS

ACKNOWLEDGMENTS
i

PREFACE: GLYPHS IN THE MEMETIC AGE
1

CHAPTER 1: DEFINING MEMES
13

CHAPTER 2: THE ACTIVE LAYERS
OF MEMETIC COMMUNICATION
40

CHAPTER 3: THE MEMETIC STRUCTURES
OF COMMUNITIES AND COLLECTIVES
70

CHAPTER 4: MEMES & GESTALT THEORY
96

CHAPTER 5: MEMETIC CREATIVE CONTENT
119

CHAPTER 6: INDUSTRIAL MEMES
140

CHAPTER 7: MEMES AS A COMMUNICATIVE ACT
161

CHAPTER 8: MEMES AS A PERFORMANCE ACT
192

CHAPTER 9: MEMES AS A SOCIOLOGICAL ACT
209

CHAPTER 10: MEMES AS A THERAPEUTIC ACT
238

POSTSCRIPT: THE DEATH AND
EVOLUTION OF MEMETIC CONTENT
260

PREFACE: GLYPHS IN THE MEMETIC AGE

Comprehending Internet culture requires a person to understand how one connects with others on a social, cultural, and psychological level. Interactions within the online realm will often cross over to the physical world as discussions maintained through computers do not remain there. People bring their beliefs, values, attitudes, and behaviors from their daily existence to the various websites and services that make up one's virtual personality and presence. This acknowledgment of the reality of modern communication and relationships mean that the way people express their realities and reactions online is worth the time and critical examination of scholars and students of Internet culture.

It is in this spirit that I wondered what future anthropologists and cultural scholars would say about these interactions. A person who goes by the Twitter handle @beach_fox looked at two generations of Internet content and created a series of minimalistic glyphs to represent the type of communication that occurred online during certain timeframes. The first series (the "Elder Glyphs") reflect the late 1990s to early 2000s popular works online.

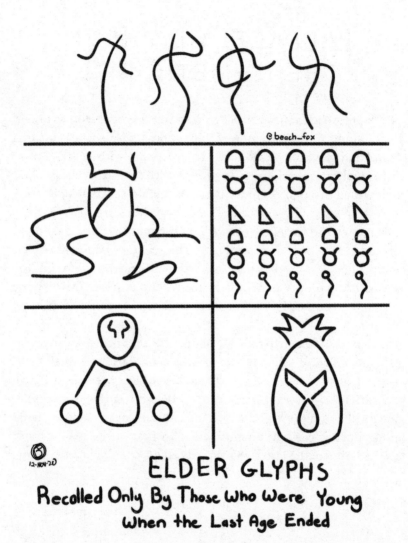

ELDER GLYPHS
Recalled Only By Those Who Were Young
When the Last Age Ended

Figure 1: Elder Glyphs by @beach_fox. They are (from top to bottom and left to right) "Dancing Baby," "All Your Base," "Hamster Dance," Strong Bad from "Homestar Runner," and "Evil Bert." Source: https://twitter.com/beach_fox/status/1327133630439837698

The last of these graphics referenced in the previous figure illustrates a key theme in introducing one of the classic works of media scholarship, Henry Jenkins' (2006) *Convergence Culture*. Jenkins used "Evil Bert" as an entry point to describe the role transmediation played in the media economy at the beginning of the 21st century. Jenkins defined **transmediation** as content creators' ability to examine works of popular culture and repurpose those works to produce a newer piece of media. Content creators are speaking in the media's language. They use the aesthetic principles and practices they learned through the cultural osmosis of being dropkicked into a society ruled by mass communication organizations.

Bert is traditionally presented as a Sesame Street character that allows children to learn how to socialize. "Evil Bert" is a transmediated version of the Sesame Street character shown supporting Hitler, the Ku Klux Klan, and Osama bin Laden (Poster, 2003). It was that repurposing of Bert's personality from a friendly character to a psychopathic monster that led media scholars to examine shifts in social messaging from the traditional broadcast medium of television to the adaptive communication system of the Internet.

The common aspect among these Elder Glyphs referenced in the first figure is that all five works are performative. The presentation of those works is similar to other pieces of content shown on broadcast channels. The original content creator crafted the work, and the content entertained the audience. Audiences could not change the overall message created by that artist. The underlying message is static and essentially unchanged over the decades since the artists created these legacies of the original visual Internet.

Another aspect to recognize in this grouping is how they all fit the criteria of a glyph. Glyphs are essentially pictographs that express an element of society as a snapshot of their cultural legacy. They are simple forms of expression with a limited range of significant meaning to the broader community of passive viewers of those works. Compare the passive nature of these first works to the second figure of glyphs.

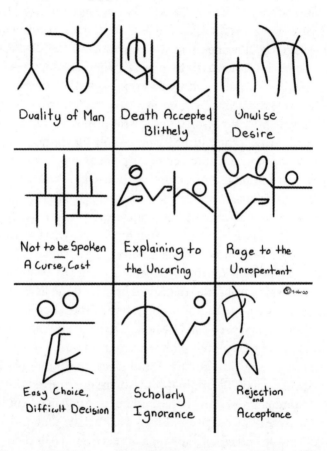

Figure 2: A collection of common glyphs of the poorly understood Memeorite civilization of the Second Silicon Age by @beach_fox. They are (from top to bottom and left to right) "Virgin vs. Chad," "Ralph In Danger," "Distracted Boyfriend," "Lost," "Me Explaining to My Mom," "Woman Yelling at Cat," "Daily Struggle," "Is This a Pigeon?," and "Drakeposting." Source: https://twitter.com/beach_fox/status/1325668490431246336?s=12

A point to note about this collection of Internet staples is this broad interpretation of what those glyphs mean to the audience. The tweet reinforces this idea of a lack of comprehensive understanding by stating, "Memeorite glyphs possess multiple conflicting interpretations and a complexity of meaning impossible to capture in a few short words. These are rough translations only." Meaningful communication and interactions use these various glyphs listed above as a starting point to address the day's issues, express various opinions to the community, and react to events in real time. That is the nature of Internet communication via social networks today. Interpretations of these symbols require a collective understanding of the complexity of the messaging. They are more than just the rough composite of various media forms superimposed on top of one another.

MEMES AS COMMUNICATIVE ACTS

Communication via online systems means that social network members imbue the regularly used symbols with collective meaning. This meaning in the digital realm lacks the traditional non-verbals that make up most of the modes of engagement within real world interactions (Maloney, Freeman, & Wohn, 2020). These symbols maintain a collective meaning among the online community members to express a personal opinion, address the community's current state, defend against conflict, or entertain others.

Meme Life: The Social, Cultural, and Psychological Aspects of Memetic Communication is meant to be a critical overview of how these cultural pieces define modern online existence. A book of this nature needs to recognize the previous contributions to the field and expand on what we know. I am indebted to the past scholarship of Ryan Milner and Limor Shifman in their attempts to provide clarity regarding the significance of the digital works that some would call "silly nonsense," "a waste of time," "a fad," or even "complete garbage." Their writing on this subject is foundational for the course I teach on this subject. My students have found the work accessible and to be a great starting point for classroom discussion. I hope to continue to follow Milner and Shifman's lead in this crucial conversation.

The one reason that I find study memes useful is that they act as the digital signposts of social discourse online and in the real world. My friends often find memes and ask me if I've seen them before. We talk about where they were found and how they were used. The conversation allows my friends to be part of the inside jokes online and share that understanding with others (Park, 2020).

This attempt to ground memes to their social significance goes beyond identifying them as mere concepts that are virally transmitted rapidly within a community or broader society. Memes are rhetorical, as they express the logical, emotional, and ethical states of the people using them. They allow a person to condense a problem facing the world and reframe it to change the perspective on the issue or provide a moment of clarity. "The Ice Bucket Challenge" is one such reframing. It took a medical condition that was not widely understood and made it more accessible by allowing people to experience the muscle stiffness associated with Lou Gehrig's disease, or amyotrophic lateral sclerosis (ALS). A by-product of this awareness was the fundraising that led to some treatments for this disease (Sherman and Wedge, 2017). The complex series of symptoms associated with this dreaded disease is simplified to garner a more precise public understanding.

MEMES AS SOCIOLOGICAL ACTS

It is also fair to argue that memes are also sociological. They act as the platform for collective expression and maintaining the norms of a given community. Memes reflect the community's social standards and act as signposts of acceptable and unacceptable interactions within the group. Suppose humor is a reasonable means of addressing the needs of a collective. In that case, memes can help members of a given community understand what modes of expression are appropriate and how to interact with one another (Gal, 2019). A simple example of memes' sociological nature can be found in the Reddit group r/SpeedOfLobster, which uses the same snapshot of a show as a starting point for collective conversations.

Figure 3.a: A graphical representation of the visual artifact used for all r/SpeedOfLobsters memes. (Holly McCoy)

The image acts as a canvas for others to display their worldly experiences. A number of the ten words are blacked out to reflect the content creator's feelings and knowledge. This simple act reshapes a single line of humorous dialogue to communicate something from the vast expanse of the human condition.

Figure 3.b: One of the r/SpeedOfLobsters memes. Original Source: https://knowyourmeme.com/photos/1411750-i-do-not-control-the-speed-at-which-lobsters-die#trending-bar (Holly McCoy)

MEMES AS PSYCHOLOGICAL ACTS

The least understood aspect of memetic interaction is that they are psychological. Memes give the content creator some form of agency to address internal conflicts with society and themselves. The crafting of mediated works into memes online allows the community to understand community members' needs, wants, desires, beliefs, values, attitudes, and behaviors. It reveals public personal reflection that the meme creator is not always aware of.

This in-depth description of meme creators' psychological state is not meant to be considered a form of treatment nor a critical analysis of a person's mental state. Instead, this acknowledgment helps foster healthy communication that psychological professionals can apply to their practices. Clinical practitioners of psychology (of which I am not one) should seek out additional tools for engagement with clients. I believe that talking about memes in a therapeutic session could lead to more open dialogues between a client and their therapist.

REFLECTING ON MEMETIC RESEARCH

This book's chapters will address the communicative, sociological, and psychological perspectives of memes as the discussion point for further research, academic conversations, and public discourse about the subject. It was crafted to be a textbook for my Memetic Communication (now Memes and Society) course. One of the struggles I had when teaching this course was finding a book that could provide a foundational place to start classroom discussions. My plan for this book is to use it to supplement Limor Shifman's (2014) *Memes in Digital Culture* and Ryan M. Milner's (2018) *The*

World Made Meme: Public Conversations and Participatory Media.
I still believe that these two books should form the foundations of scholarship in the field of memes. My entry into this field will hopefully expand the scholarship beyond the sociological implications of this work. It seems fair to address the psychological aspects, too, in order to develop additional branches extending from the solid roots that Shifman and Milner laid down. I was hoping the classic text *Culture in Networks* by Paul McLean (2016) would fulfill some of those missing areas of focus from the other two books. It is a great graduate school level of review of the areas of network interactions, but sadly, it is too in-depth of a study of the materials. This book cannot possibly do the justice that McLean did in describing network interactions that would relate to a class on memes. This book will refer to McLean's text to enhance these descriptions.

One of the reasons I think McLean's work made sense to add to my class was due to McLean's ability to perform a deep-dive into the heart of key theoretical issues. Since most of my earlier research has been in the field of cybernetics, it seems logical that my definition of knowledge falls within the realm of cybernetic epistemology. Cybernetic epistemology is defined through a system model. People are the main drivers of this system, as they connect with nodes (events, groups, other individuals and/or non-human sentient units) on the network through a series of roads (the exchange of information or other interactions between nodes) where all elements of the network are awareness of the changes that are happening to other aspects of the network (e.g., social unrest shutting down parts of the network, trending topics highlighting what the network thinks is important, or an influencer driving traffic to their YouTube channel). Memes in this model are the after-expressions of this knowledge within the community.

I will be presenting several case studies within this book that reflect the cybernetic epistemology related to meme studies. This focus on case studies should more critically apply McLean's text to the realm of memes instead of the public networks of the Internet. All cases come from the last two years of teaching Memetic Communication.

I include references about a theorist at the end of each of the first series of chapters to show how the materials in this book connect with scholarship in other fields of study. The coursework for Memetic Communication was interdisciplinary. Therefore, bringing in academics with diverse experiences will help show how memetic scholarship fits within different academic disciplines. The researchers selected to conclude the chapters provide an excellent coda to the perspectives explored in those chapters.

It also seemed appropriate to expand this work beyond the classroom setting. Two additional audiences should find use in the words contained in this book. The first of these two audiences are mental health professionals that would like to use digital works like memetic content in therapeutic sessions with clients. This secondary audience will find value in applying the praxis and the theory within the chapters to regular interactions with those seeking better mental health. With that audience in mind, each chapter concludes with a therapeutic consideration to apply memetic communication to a session with a client.

Finally, a general audience interested in memetic content and its impact on society and culture will appreciate learning how the meme's definitions have evolved over the term's history. The biological introduction of memes to describe small units of cultural information has dramatically changed in the Internet era. We will take the time to explore and dissect memetic content to better understand the messaging and its mode of engaging with online audiences.

Works Cited

Maloney, D., Freeman, G., & Wohn, D. Y. (2020). "Talking without a Voice": Understanding non-verbal communication in social virtual reality. *Proceedings of the ACM on Human-Computer Interaction, 4*(CSCW2), 1-25.

McLean, P. (2016). *Culture in Networks*. John Wiley & Sons.

Milner, R. M. (2018). *The World Made Meme: Public conversations and participatory media*. Information Society Series.

Park, S. K. (2020, February). Understanding Usage of Memes Over Social Medias Through Semantics: A survey. In *2020 IEEE 14th International Conference on Semantic Computing* (ICSC) (pp. 387-392). IEEE.

Russell, D., & Ison, R. (2017). Fruits of Gregory Bateson's Epistemological Crisis: Embodied mind-making and interactive experience in research and professional praxis. *Canadian Journal of Communication, 42*(3), 485-514.

Sherman, C., & Wedge, D. (2017). *The Ice Bucket Challenge: Pete Frates and the fight against ALS*. University Press of New England.

Shifman, L. (2014). *Memes in Digital Culture*. MIT Press.

CHAPTER 1:
DEFINING MEMES

I t is in the nature of people to push the envelope of what communication technologies can do. Novels are the ultimate example of what the printing press could produce. Live news reports via the radio became the way that most families learned about the world in the early part of the 20th century. Television's trademark contribution to the cultural development of society was the miniseries (Tucker & Shah, 1992; Brown & Singhal, 1990; Kyrchanoff, 2020). Online communication is no different. The regular use of animated GIFs marked earlier Internet and email culture as a mode of expression.

Social media has two such communication constructions. You-Tube allowed people to add embedded videos to websites. Many social media services like Facebook and Twitter co-opted this communication mode in later versions of their sites. People share all aspects of their lives for an audience ranging from a few people to millions. All videos serve the same purpose. The videomakers can capture their experiences and view of the world, edit those captured moments to tell a coherent story, and present those edited works to an audience that cares about the content creator's work.

By its definition and functions, embedded video works the same online as on other electronic mediums, as it is the use of moving images and sounds to present a message to the audience. A more "significant form of communication" (Barnard, 2016, 65) came from when people started to use and combine various pieces of content found online to express a singular message through one file. It is this attempt to communicate those messages that are worth our time to examine.

This form, of course, is the meme.

MEMETIC TERMINOLOGY

Before addressing the thematic issues at hand, I should explain three terms that will come up later. These concepts are extensions of the definitions from this chapter but should be seen to critically examine memes at an academic and therapeutic level. The first of these terms is a memetic artifact. **Memetic artifacts** are those constructions studied by scholars and preserved for research that considers all social factors that influence that meme's development and explains how the meme is disseminated through a community. Referencing a memetic artifact means that we need to think about all of the aspects that led to a meme's use for a given situation. In the words of John Berger (2012), this critical term is not used to create a "false mystification" to make memes inaccessible, nor is it to keep the knowledge "jealously guarded and kept within the narrow preserves" of those that study memes. Memetic artifacts are referenced to reflect that they are not silly or simple. There is a process at work to create any meme, and we need to understand that. This book will attempt to guide this cause.

Secondly, the term **memetic content** will come up from time to time. This term is used as a shorthand for the process of creating a meme (from start to finish). The tools of mediated production are more easily accessible to the general public. People can craft digital masterworks with a speed and resolution unheard of two hundred years ago, or even three decades ago (Pool, 1983). This simplified content creation process is made more accessible through smartphones, which have become the singular media production house. The combination of software and hardware found on most phones allows for immediacy of expression while maintaining a semi-professional quality to the produced works.

Memetic communication is the final term to address now. The use of a meme is not a standalone process. Memes are the symbols that allow for exchanging information or acting as part of a series of meaningful interactions. That last statement is a pretty good definition of communication (Tilton, 2020). It is an active process that the meme creator, the meme user, and the rest of the community take part in.

MEME AS CULTURAL TRANSMITTER

Scholars in the field define this fundamental term in a few ways. One of the first scholars to use the term "meme" to describe cultural interactions was Richard Dawkins. Dawkins (2016) is a cultural theorist that borrowed this idea from biological studies in 1976. His development of this concept focused on the smallest presentation of cultural information that could "convey the idea of a unit of cultural transmission, or a unit of imitation" (352). Cultural memes, unlike their biological counterparts, mutate through human creativity instead of random changes. Memes change by others' actions within social networks and present a different viewpoint to the broader community than the one expressed initially by the meme's first producer. These units are defined and examined through cultural paradigms that create a series of fragmented "shared social experiences" and distributed via some form of a social network to represent the norms of a given community and the beliefs/values of an individual.

Shared social experiences often refer to those aspects of social interactions and communal conduct in which members of a given society:

1. feel a sense of belonging to one another through the elements of an event, location, time, or cultural work,

2. that sense of belonging allows those who experienced the event, location, time, or cultural work to bond over their experiences,

3. those experiences are detached from the ordinary experiences that the members of a society would experience in their daily interactions with others,

4. the elements of that event, location, time, or cultural work allows you commune with others,

5. the element of that event, location, time, or cultural work allows a member of society to connect in a meaningful way with others, and

6. the members of society who experience that event, location, time, or cultural work discuss it with others in a friendly and pleasant manner (Rihova, 2013).

A central theme to these six points is the idea of culture and cultural works. These concepts will come up several times in this book. Communication commentator Douglas Rushkoff (1996) (along with cultural critics Henry Jenkins, Tara McPherson, and Jane Shattuc (2002)) have a tough time defining culture as it evades a simple, all-embracing description. Our view of culture shifts rapidly. People are immersed in the by-products of culture daily. All aspects of culture belong to the people living in a society. Those by-products (e.g., artistic works and creative pursuits) reflect the moral, spiritual, and aesthetic standards of a given community. Memes would seem to fit this description of a cultural work.

MEMES AS ALLEGORICAL COMMUNICATION

Sociological scholar Ian Bogost addressed this hybridization between shared social experiences and cultural communication in a 2014 *Atlantic* article entitled "Shaka, When the Walls Fell." Bogost uses the 1991 *Star Trek: The Next Generation* episode "Darmok" as a model to essentially explain allegorical communication and how this model is different from what we would generally consider communication. We will focus on a simple analysis of three types of language and communication before addressing allegorical communication as a means of setting up the significance of allegorical communication.

Idiographic (idea-centered) communication (like Aztec glyphs) represents concepts and ideas within glyphs. These language types are interpreted rather than directly read or spoken as other languages (Risager, 2018). The issue with these communication forms is that symbols within the glyphs do not graph onto a traditional lexicon. A person must be a member of a given society to understand each of the glyphs' significance. The number of glyphs are relatively small compared to other languages. Even with the small set of glyphs, these languages are more challenging to translate due to a lack of contextual information about the writing.

Logographic (image-centered) communication and languages (like Egyptian hieroglyphics) use a form of picture-writing as a simplified form of expression with their phonetic complements (e.g., the spoken form of the writing) maintaining a direct relationship to the image. This direct relationship to the image is a basic form of communication that transmits the "meaningful components of words" (Roberts & Street, 2017). Symbols can be orally expressed via the phonetic (sound-based) elements embedded in the writing. A new image can be produced to represent a concept or idea not initially incorporated in the previous lexicon.

Linear alphabetic languages (like English) break down these symbols into phonemes (the basic unit of sounds) to construct communication aspects. The consonants and vowels form the foundation of all spoken and written communication in a given society. New concepts and ideas can be easily added to a given society's lexicon via glyphs' composition to craft a new word of those concepts and ideas.

These three languages use syntactic rules to express ideas. Idiographic communication will encode ideas in a manner that is acceptable to those literate in the language. It can change when all people who use the language agree to a given set of changes. Logographic communication has a formal set of rules that tell the communicators in what order to place images for the most direct transmission of information. Alphabetic languages will have formal and informal practices grounded in social norms and a conventional education system that trains people how to communicate with others in society.

Best-selling author Mark Forsyth (2016) denotes these formal and informal practices in his book *The Elements of Eloquence*. To quote from the book:

> Adjectives in English absolutely have to be in this order: opinion-size-age-shape-colour-origin-material-purpose noun. So you can have a lovely little old rectangular green French silver whittling knife. But if you mess with that word order in the slightest you'll sound like a maniac. It's an odd thing that every English speaker uses that list, but almost none of us could write it out. And as size comes before colour, green great dragons can't exist (pg. 45).

Forsyth was referring to a story that J.R.R. Tolkien wrote when he was seven years old. Word order was the underlying theme of Forsyth's chapter. He grounds this discussion under the chapter title "hyperbaton," which is the inversion of the "normal" order of words for dramatic emphasis. The European Culture Editor from the *New York Times* Matthew Anderson (2017) tweeted the French equivalent of this rule,

> Yes, there is. You remember it 'bags': beauty, age, goodness, size.

The example described by Forsyth and Anderson gets to the heart of the three forms of communication in this section. All three are crafted with a sense of social expectation on how they can be used in society. They act as cultural tools to express what is happening in the community and to archive that information and recall it later (e.g., the written word) for long- or short-term cultural exchanges (e.g., the spoken word).

Allegorical communication (like the one analyzed by Bogost) is a form of cultural transmission that depends on a multilayered interpretation of the performative presentation. Unlike the three previously listed forms of communication, there isn't a syntactic construction for communicative acts. Instead, there is almost a social-psychological sense of ritualistic order in this mode of communication. What an allegorical method of communication loses in the precision of the moment, it gains a collective understanding of the moment. Traditional communication is mostly psychological and egotistical as it is the expression of personal experience through the selection of self-constructed statements. "I am doing well," is an example of the egotistical (first-person narrative). Even when the speaker uses second- or third-person narratives in their communication, it comes from the speaker's perspective of the reality of the situation.

As demonstrated by the examples from *Darmok*, metaphors and stories advance communication interactions. "Kadir beneath Mo Moteh" is used to express one party's failure to under-stand another party's communication. It is this underlying mode of expression that allows for meaningful information to be trans-mitted. Memes use similar metaphors (through mediated works and narratives) to express meaningful information between people. The parallels are so strong between memetic communication and the language in "Darmok" that memes have been created using the scenes from "Darmok" in what can be described as a proto-meme.

Figure 4: An example of a Darmok proto-meme created by David Servo and posted on the TPM Meme Research and Development Facebook group. (Source: https://www.facebook.com/photo?fbid=3 571433886259532&set=gm.4304124982942662)

MEMES AS THE TRANSMITTERS OF MEANINGFUL INFORMATION

Both Bogost and Dawkins address a critical aspect of defining the concept and addressing memes' overall effectiveness. Crafting and posting memes requires the transmission of information that is meaningful to the community. Meaningful information becomes encoded within the meme when the content creator crafts a message that addresses the interests, needs, and concerns of a community to the point that the meme resonates with the community at large. In this example, information is simply a thread of individual data points that the creator put together that the audience can use to get a different perspective on the world (Theirauf, 1999).

Viewers of a memetic work can find meaning when the meme has elements of popular culture acting as a reflection of the social network's communal reality (either online or in the real world) and as a reflection of viewers' personal experiences. Popular culture elements within the memes can also connect with the viewer's logical interpretation of the world, their emotional state, or even how they see their relationship with others within the community, especially if they recall the references to the relevant shows, titles, or performances and how they relate to their interpretations, emotional states, or relationships.

Dawkins' definition also introduces that memes can imitate other popular culture works. As a creative technique, imitation allows somebody to duplicate the key characteristics that define popular culture by mimicking the aesthetics and messaging present in that given work. The level of reproduction that a memetic content creator uses within a given meme, according to Dawkins, allows the memetic content creator to be more subtle and complex in their presentation of their message within the meme. These "variations of a theme" are grounded in the memetic content creator's ability to identify what makes a popular culture work unique in the audience's mind. It is also these variations of a theme that lead us to another definition of memes.

BLACKMORE'S DEFINITION: MEMES AS AN IMITATION OF REALITY

Susan Blackmore dug into more details on this concept in her book, *The Meme Machine* (2000). One of the critical aspects of her argument is that "when you imitate someone else, something is passed on. This "something" can then be passed on again, and again, and so take on a life of its own" (pg. 3). Blackmore's "something" can be a cultural truth, a universal certainty, or a personal point of reflection. She goes on by noting the medium of the "something" can be passed on to others (e.g., songs, catchphrases, images, clothing trends) becomes successful through an "evolutionary algorithm" in which the result of moving through society leads to a "complex, chaotic, and unpredictable" conclusion. This conclusion is predictable in one aspect, however. The whole of the "something" is lost in the transmission and translation as it moves through communication and interaction networks. What remains is an imperfect imitation of what was originally expressed, much like when a person makes a copy of a copy of a copy of a copy of a copy on a copier that the final result is a low-quality image when compared to the original work.

These transmissions of cultural significance that Blackmore is addressing are fundamentally connected to the way we learn about the world. She points to the idea of social learning ("learning that is influenced by observing, or interacting with, another animal or person" (pg. 47)) as a means of reacting to the world to find what is valuable and useful to mimic. Blackmore is mainly focusing on value and usefulness in real-world interactions, as opposed to online interactions, due to the primitive nature of the Internet during the time that Blackmore wrote her book.

She denotes three issues related to using memes to imitate reality. Blackmore explains that setting the boundaries of the given memetic is not easy to commonly define as people pick up on different aspects of the "something" that others can reliably replicate and use as a springboard to create newer "somethings" in society. The second problem with real world memes is that it is hard to nail down how people are able to remember and perform or create the aspects of the meme that are worth repeating. Blackmore crafts an explanation of this issue that I am choosing to simplify as the neural networks that make up human brains are complex structures that we still do not fully understand. Finally, future memes inherit some (but not all) of the aspects of their previous generations. The alterations between generations impact how the "something" is understood by those who replicate the meme and those viewing the replication. She (along with others) refers to this ability to inherit a series of common characteristics as **Lamarckian**. These characteristics are replicated in cultural memes by the communities deciding which parts of a given meme are worth repeating in future generations.

Social learning is related to these three issues of memes, as it forces both parties to transmit memetic knowledge to recognize that there can be multiple aspects within a cultural work that are useful or valuable to repeat. We may not immediately understand why they are useful or valuable, but some cultural works are more appreciated by the community. This idea of social learning is also part of the creation of online memes as they use the wisdom of the crowd to determine what memes are more popular within the network. Content creators will repeat those techniques until they are no longer popular or accepted by the community. The development of these techniques sped up online with the development of the Internet.

SHIFMAN'S DEFINITION: MEMES AS COLLECTIVE EXPRESSIONS

One of the first scholars (along with Jean Burgess, Colin Lankshear, Michele Knobel, and Lance Bennett) to examine digital works online as memes was Limor Shifman. She begins her analysis of the term in her book *Memes in Digital Culture* (2014) by using the concept's prevalent perception. "The tag 'Internet meme' is commonly applied to describe the propagation of items such as jokes, rumors, videos, and websites from person to person via the Internet" (pg. 1). The concern with this definition of memes is that it is not discrete enough to distinguish a meme from other forms of Internet communication and interactions.

Shifman expands on this starting point of a definition by addressing how intertextuality drives memes beyond this basic concept. Intertextuality is how different pieces of content relate to one another as they all exist within society's same cultural aspects. She denotes that memes will "often relate to each other in complex, creative, and surprising ways" (pg. 2) to show this standard connection between cultural works. Intertextuality is also the means by which everyday users of the Internet can express themselves. Memes are a canvas that people can use to explain their thoughts, opinions, viewpoints, and knowledge to the entire community. Those modes of expression are vital for Internet communication. They allow users in various Internet communities (social media services, user groups, message boards, or any other online collective) to "speak" using similar composition modes. Shirman argues that the Internet's intertextual nature led to a more hypermemetic, logical approach to online communication and interactions. Specifically, she indirectly argues that memes depend on the viewer having some cultural literacy, as they often directly reference other popular culture works (books, graphic novels, games, movies, etc.). This knowledge will influence the audience's interpretation of that meaningful information within the meme.

The hypermemetic state of memes becomes clear as Shifman expresses one of the better definitions of a meme: "a group of digital items sharing common characteristics... which were created with awareness of each other, and were circulated, imitated, and/or transformed via the Internet by many users" (pg. 41). The awareness of memes speaks to the communal knowledge related to the role memes play in society. The collective expression that this definition suggests is that people understand that there is an original act that can be modified in a performance by others to transform the underlying message of the work. The underlying message is also the "something" that Blackmore refers to in her definition of memes.

Shifman's final point in her analysis of memes is that we should consider memes different from viral content. Viral works typically are spread at an incredible speed via personal recommendations from social media friends that can expand beyond the original one-on-one interactions. There can only be a singular viral work with one message delivered to millions of people. Viral content does not allow for adaptation or manipulation.

Simply stated, others cannot remix a viral video.

MILNER'S DEFINITION: MEMES AS THE ARTIFACTS OF THE REMIX CULTURE

Ryan Milner (2016) pushes Shifman's discussion of memes' remixability further in his book *The World Made Meme*. He argues that memes are more than one mediated work. Rather, memes only exist as they are "aggregate text, collectively created, circulated, and transformed by countless cultural participants" (pg. 17). Milner points to Shifman's definition as he denotes "in their common characteristics, mutual awareness, and transformative circulation, memes are at once universal and particular, familiar and foreign" (pg. 30) as a reason that they speak to us and are more expressive than any one post created by someone on a social network. It is our ability to use this work as an amplification of the "something" that we wish to express. He continues on to explain that "they're small expressions with big implications."

The "big implications" that Milner refers to only come about by disseminating the work within a social network and allowing others to play with the central messaging within the memetic content. It is their interplay that forms the heart of Milner's underlying definition of memes. Milner states the memes are "multimodal texts that facilitate participation by reappropriation, by balancing a fixed premise with novel expression" (ibid) as they allow for complex ideas to be effectively transmitted to others who share the same social networks. He grounds his definition in a meme's ability to help facilitate participation by simply sharing content within a social network and society at large.

Milner points to five ways that memes aid content-driven participation within communities. Memes are more than the disseminators of information; rather, memes allow people to code multiple messages within that content that represent a complicated conversation within computer-aided communication. It is this characteristic of memes that Milner would call their **multimodality**. People within these social networks are influenced by the books and graphic novels they read, the music they listen to, and the television shows and movies they watch. Popular works are **reappropriated** when they are adapted to present a different message or "something" than what was in the original work. Adapted works only become memes when the messages within the crafted work "connect with enough participants to inspire iteration after iteration" from that adapted work. This level of connection means that the adapted work **resonates** with others. Beyond the messaging connecting with others, the adapted works shared some common characteristics with other similar works that speak to the experiences of a community of users of these works. It is the common characteristics and the connection with an organization population that Milner calls the meme's **collectivism**. Finally, a meme is only a meme if it is shared or **spread** to others.

Milner's perception of memes (as of the time his book was published) is based on a sociological construction of this central concept. Memes can really only exist as a hybrid between the underlying message within the memes and the audience that is there to observe the meme. Shifman's work on this subject also seems to put the weight on the concept based on the social adaption of the content itself. The social observation of the meme has been deemed more important than the act of creation. It is here that I want to propose a slightly different way of thinking about memes.

HER'S DEFINITION: MEMES AS A STATE OF SOCIAL INTERACTION

One of the first questions that get asked in the study of memes is how to categorize them. The argument that it is a means of organizing memes will lead to a better sense of how they help with social interactions. Shifman set the foundation of this discussion with her description of the "Four Phases of Memetic Works." She addresses the original context, which acts as the primary spark of memetic action. **Original context** gives content creators a canvas to which to add creative elements for further creative expressions. The most common additional creative expression is simply **mimicking** (a direct performance or replication of the original context) or **remixing** (adapting the original context for a different purpose, platform, occasion, or audience) to become a new memetic artifact within a social network. Once the original context goes through a series of remixes or mimicries, it is placed within the "marketplace of ideas." Once a critical mass of people uses this memetic artifact, it has survived the process's **competition/selection** phase. Finally, the memetic artifact's performance can exist in the real world as most people recognize what is being represented in the performance. The memetic artifact eventually becomes **hypermemetic** when it crosses over the digital to non-digital performance space.

A deeper dive into this categorizing to understand how memes aid in social interactions comes from the work of Seong-Young Her, Jeremy Cahill, Masha Zharova, Mikhail Conrad Nacua, Mike M., and Thomas Rososchansky at "The Philosopher's Meme" website. It is fair for me to state at this moment that the work performed by these scholars (and the auxiliary work on the /tmpg/-TPM Meme Research and Development Facebook group) goes above and beyond any work that I could do as a solo scholar in the field of memes. I want to focus on the eight "Memetic States," or what is described as the "Phylomemetic Tree of Internet Memes" from "The Philosopher's Meme" as a means of making a more extended argument about memetic definitions. **Phylomemetics** refers to the creation of a model of a tree that places various cultural entities on the model based on historical trends and evolutionary relationship (Tyler, 2011).

The most elemental state of any meme is the meme as an idea or **gene**. In this state, the meme is merely an expression of a singular cultural thought or social truth. Her (2016) refers to these types of memes as traditionalist, as they are standalone works that can be easily copied and reproduced on a wide variety of platforms.

This is essentially the starting point for all memetic content. It is where a content creator attempts to express a meaningful message within the structure of a meme.

Most of the memes used by the average person (or as Her would refer to them, a "normie") would fit the meme as an **object**. There is a level of simplicity to the work as the meme is merely a record of community norms. These works help people learn memetic communication grammar as the community gives feedback on using the meme correctly. This state reflects the most basic form that people would generally recognize as a meme.

There comes a point where a meme can act as a reaction to others online. It is when a meme can be used as a form of "social shorthand" to express or describe complex social or cultural themes to a general public that the meme becomes a **trope**. This state happens when a meme is often used for a particular situation online that the meaning of the meme is associated with that situation. The meme is so clearly presented that it allows all involved to imagine the social aspects related to the meme based on how the person used the meme and why it was used. We are trained to read memes this way (e.g., reaction memes). Tropes also express the "inside jokes" of the Internet as they reference the themes and ideas that are central to regular online interactions.

After a meme's tropic state, people will feel comfortable playing around with the meme's structure and its elements. It is at this point that people will recognize that the work is **conceptually** a meme. People will start to, according to Her, subvert the conventions that make up the meme's humor and ironically use the meme as a form of social interaction and communication. It is in this memetic state that most of the novel creativity of the medium arises. Memes will be interjected into other ones to create newer forms of expression. It is also important to note that this state is the first one in which the meme evolves a simple form of expression (either thematically or contextually, as described above).

The mash-up of memetic artifacts sometimes makes it easier to transmit additional cultural or sociological information to others. It is in this way that the meme acts as a **vessel** for that transmission. These memes will often reference other memes or works of popular culture as the source of the humor within the meme. It takes multiple cultural knowledge types (both memetic and popular culture) to "unlock" all of the meanings from these types of memes.

There is also a point where a meme becomes a platform and canvas for engagement among a community during a period of time. It is here that the meme becomes ritualistic in nature. Flash mobs are one example of this type of **ritualistic** memetic state or **event** that allows the community to co-create a sense of meaning within the memetic performance. Participants of this memetic action are grounded in a cultural-rooted performance as a mode of expression.

The last two Memetic States are more meta in nature. **Functional** memes are those in which the creator delivers their message using a more "guttural" presentation of cultural information. It is a primary communication and interaction model that allows the meme creator to present non-ironic work online that is so complex that it cannot easily be adapted for mainstream culture.

Finally, meme creators can craft memes that simply comment on memes in general. These memetic **critiques** provide a platform to recognize and discuss memes as a mode of social interaction. They also offer a meta-analysis to either make fun of less complex memes, deconstruct the meme-making process, or regress to the point of incomprehensibility. Meta-analyses within the memes address the community's concerns with any template, layer element, or memes as a whole.

TILTON'S DEFINITION: MEMES AS MULTILAYERED MEDIATED MARKS ON THE WORLD

I believe that Her's understanding of the meme is fair but fails to simplify the central characteristics that define a meme. Therefore, considering all of the previous literature and research on the subject, I propose a newer definition of memes. Memes are active, multilayered communication constructions that are influenced by social factors and represent a mode of individual expression, in which meaning-making is controlled by both a community that understands that the whole of the work is greater than the sum of its parts and a collective that places that creative content into some part of the broader cultural industry embedded in society. There are a few reasons that this definition better captures the spirit of what a meme is.

We should first recognize the role of the meme creator in this process. It is fair to argue that the previous definitions seem to remove the content creator's part from the process. Their interpretation of the world is what is transmitted within the meme. It is also what the rest of the community is reacting to or against.

The meme's multilayered nature also gives the meme creator "agency" within the community to express themselves while maintaining a given society's norms. A limited number of avenues are available for typical people to address the world or represent a more extensive position for the rest of the community to consider. Memes are also active in this way as the meme itself can express counterpositions from its original context.

It is also significant to note that the previous attempts to define a meme fail to adequately address how the memes' pieces speak to the collective message within the meme. This failure is not the fault of any of the brilliant scholars listed above; rather, this point seems to have been overlooked due to memes' overwhelming power to express compelling points on their own.

The final defense of this definition comes from recognizing the two groups that relate to the transmission of this work. The concepts of community and collective are both borrowed from others. **Community** comes from Ferdinand Tönnies' (2017) *Community and Society* in which he discusses how communities are composed of people who interact with one another and share intimate and private knowledge of others with whom they interact regularly. Paul McLean's (2017) definition of a **collective** works in this discussion as it addresses a series of characteristics that bind a group of people or grouping of cultural works together.

It is fair to note in this part of the description that one term that will come up often in this book might be considered confusing. That term is mediated content. **Mediated** content refers to the end-product of a content creation process that incorporates more than just text or a single image. It is a composite of text, graphics (both photographic and artistically crafted), audio, video, animation, and computer-aided communication. The term is meant to act as a reminder of the complexity of memes. Authors translate the thoughts in their brain to words that become a bridge of understanding that moves an idea from one person to another. Artists use the medium (or mediums) they are most comfortable with to leave an impression on an audience in the form of an artistic expression. Mediated content has the benefit of both being an authored work that transmits ideas through the combination of mediums, where the end-result would be considered an artistic expression.

The nuance of the distinction between these two concepts helps explain memes' effectiveness as a transmitter of information and how these mediated works help with personal expressions. These distinct elements will be explored as we examine individual memes throughout this book.

WHY DO MEMES MATTER AND ARE WORTH OUR TIME STUDYING?

It might be fair to ask, after that comprehensive deep-dive into the definition of memes, to address the issue of why memes are worth this much academic and clinical focus. They may seem to be jokes that you share online, ways of presenting facts to your friends, or even the means of explaining what is happening within your community. These simplistic purposes get to the heart of why memes matter. They effectively perform aspects of communication using multimedia assets. It is the perfect synthesis of Internet interactions. This acknowledgment of their perfect quality is not to suggest that memes deliver truthful or accurate information. Instead, their compositional nature allows for a saturation of knowledge that can overwhelm the viewer and speak to the community's sensibilities. A community's sensibilities are the second reason that memes are worth studying.

A critical examination of memetic content offers the researcher a better understanding of what the community in which the content was posted considers acceptable, what they will not tolerate, and what they think is the best expression of who they are. Jeff Howe (2006) described the nature of Internet interactions by explaining the four themes that drive content creation. The first: user-generated content represents most of the work that people see online (as opposed to professional content or even content that reflects messaging from an organization). This means that the creative output online comes from community members. Crowdsourced works are the second theme, which means that the community creates these formal and informal requests for content that reflect the community's state of being and creative tastes, and community members produce those works in response. A third theme is that communities naturally divide themselves into subcommunities based on a series of niche and specialized characteristics that define their members.

Howe's last theme is the most useful to think about when considering the value of studying memes. He addresses the theme of folksonomy. A basic definition of folksonomy is a means that a community uses to organize content and fans of that content. Defining creative categories (e.g., musical genres), adding metadata to the files (e.g., composers and comments about the work), and tagging works (e.g., using keywords or tags to describe content) are the three common ways that folksonomies exist online. A fourth manner by which a community organizes content – one that is often overlooked – is the reactions and comments via social networks. User recommendations drive community interest towards some content. Memes are the perfect example of the folksonomy that Howe is referring to in his article. Sites like Know Your Meme and Imgur help people develop categories, metadata, and tags for memes. The rest of the Internet allows all of us to react to and comment about our favorite memes online. One just need to see most Facebook feeds to notice the amount of memes that we collectively share and respond to in the comments.

The final defense for the value of studying memetic content is that memes speak to a person's psychological state as much as they reflect what is happening in the community. Art (which should include memes) is grounded in the personal. It represents a person's political, religious, and moral statements as much as it exhibits their artistic, creative, and technical talents. To ignore that truth means ignoring the door into an artist's mind. Memes alone do not allow psychological professionals to diagnose mental issues. These creative works should be seen as a gateway to address more profound matters a person has and is unwilling to talk about.

LOOKING AHEAD

Now that we have established a thorough discourse for how to talk about memes, we need to focus on the more significant task of applying memes in a sociological, communicative, and (most importantly for this book) psychological framework. They will form the primary themes for the rest of this book.

Chapters two through six will address the aspects of the definitions described in the first chapter. The memetic examples presented in those chapters will reinforce critical points raised to make the denser theory more accessible. One of the significant criticisms of past writing about memes is the rigorous academic language used to explain central memetic concepts. This book will follow the example set by John Berger and demystify these mediated works.

Chapters seven through ten will dig into social science theory to examine how the definitions shaped by the first six chapters of the book reflect what is happening online (through social networking services) and the real world (through social interactions). These short primers of the psychology, communication, and sociology literature are not a complete overview of the entire scope of those disciplines. Only the relevant research on memes and Internet culture will be addressed in those chapters.

It seems fitting to conclude this book with one of the discussions that always come up during the last weeks of the course that I teach on this subject matter. The postscript will focus on the lifecycle of a meme, in order to approach the "death of the meme" as part of more substantial social interactions that occur online. This analysis seeks to go beyond the codas of communication to the point of understanding when a meme no longer speaks to an individual's experiences, beliefs, values, or attitudes.

Each of the first six chapters will discuss therapeutic considerations that psychological professionals might want to address during a clinical session with a client. The rationale for this addition is more than introducing a point of praxis to this writing. One of the areas lacking in previous literature on memes is finding an angle that professionals could use to apply the research to everyday practice. The questions at the end of these chapters will guide how to best approach this subject with clients.

The first series of questions have a visual communication influence. This chapter's focusing questions are designed to help psychological professionals sense the important contextual information from memes, select what contextual information is worth discussing with a client, and perceive the separation point between real world experiences and online interactions of the client. A psychological professional should ground these conversations to have a better understanding of a client's interactions online. An excellent place to start seems to be to talk with them and ask them to share two or three memes that they use regularly. The framing question that is best suited to advance the conversation is:

1.   What about this meme speaks to you?

One of the insights gained by asking this question gets to the client's beliefs and values. This engagement might reveal deeper issues to address in later sessions.

It all depends on maintaining an open dialogue about the nature of the work they are sharing. Next one might ask:

2.   How do you use this meme?

Answering this question allows the client to reflectively analyze how they communicate online, what communities they belong to online, and their relationship with other community members.

If the client is creating memes regularly, psychological professionals can get to the heart of the memetic content they are making by asking:

3. What inspired the creation of the meme?

This question will focus on their creative process, how they view the communities they belong to online, and their overall view of society. Productive dialogues related to these questions depend on psychological professionals focusing on those definitions of memes addressed in this chapter.

Works Cited

Anderson, M. (2017, January 06). Yes, there is. You remember it 'bags': Beauty, age, goodness, size. Retrieved November 28, 2020, from https://twitter.com/MattAndersonNYT/status/817309403561029632

Barnard, S. R. (2016). Spectacles of Self(ie) Empowerment? Networked Individualism and the Logic of the (Post)Feminist Selfie. *Communication and Information Technologies Annual, 11*, 63–88. https://doi.org/10.1108/s2050-206020160000011014

Berger, J. (2012, October 08). *Ways of Seeing, Episode 1 (1972)*. Retrieved December 06, 2020, from https://www.youtube.com/watch?v=0pDE4VX_9Kk

Blackmore, S., (2000). *The Meme Machine (Vol. 25). Oxford Paperbacks.*

Brown, W. J., & Singhal, A. (1990). Ethical dilemmas of prosocial television. *Communication Quarterly, 38*(3), 268-280.

Bogost, I. (2014, June 18). *Shaka, When the Walls Fell*. Retrieved November 28, 2020, from https://www.theatlantic.com/entertainment/archive/2014/06/star-trek-tng-and-the-limits-of-language-shaka-when-the-walls-fell/372107/

Dawkins, R. (2016). *The Selfish Gene (40th Anniversary Edition). Oxford University Press.*

Forsyth, M. (2013). *The Elements of Eloquence: How to turn the perfect English phrase*. Icon Books Ltd.

Howe, J. (2006, December 17). *Your Web, Your Way*. Retrieved December 6, 2020, from http://content.time.com/time/magazine/article/0,9171,1570815,00.html

Jenkins, H., Shattuc, J., & McPherson, T. (2003). *Hop on Pop: The politics and pleasures of popular culture.* Duke University Press.

Kyrchanoff, M. W. (2020). Inventing Nostalgia for the "Golden Age" of the National Middle Ages and Fear of the Future. *Galactica Media: Journal of Media Studies*, *2*(4), 112-151.

McLean, P. (2016). *Culture in Networks*. John Wiley & Sons.

Menosky, J. (Writer), & Kolbe, W. (Director). (1991, September 30). Darmok [Television series episode]. In *Star Trek: The Next Generation*.

Milner, R. M. (2018). *The World Made Meme: Public conversations and participatory media*. Information Society Series.

Pool, I. de S. (1983). *Technologies of Freedom*. Harvard University Press.

Risager, K. (2018). *Representations of the World in Language Textbooks*. Multilingual Matters.

Roberts, C., & Street, B. (2009). Spoken and Written Language. In F. Coulmas (Ed.), *The Handbook of Sociolinguistics* (pp. 168–186). Blackwell Publishers.

Shifman, L. (2014). *Memes in Digital Culture*. MIT Press.

Tilton, S. (2020). *The Journalism Breakdown: Writing multimedia journalism content in an era of changing media systems & economic models*. CFSC Publishing

Tönnies, F. (2017). *Community and Society*. Routledge.

Tucker, L. R., & Shah, H. (1992). Race and the transformation of culture: The making of the television miniseries Roots. *Critical Studies in Media Communication*, *9*(4), 325-336.

Tyler, T. (2011). *Memetics: Memes and the science of cultural evolution*. Mersenne Publishing.

CHAPTER 2: THE ACTIVE LAYERS OF MEMETIC COMMUNICATION

One of the sticking points in a discussion of memes is the distinction between memes and other online content. The previous chapter's definitions start to distinguish memes as more than other online displays of digital works. Academic analyses of this form of content only begin to get to the heart of this content's compelling nature. This chapter will extend the definition offered in the last chapter to point out the complex nature of this computer-mediated communication content.

Memes are different from other forms of digital content in that memes make the complicated simple through a singular display of information; other forms of digital content are just simple. A meme creator provides content that can be layered to build significant meaning to a community. Samples of popular culture content, textual information tying the pieces together, and a template that forms the meme's foundation are central to the meaning-making performed by the community that the meme is addressing. Other forms of digital content are self-contained works that speak their messages simply and clearly to be effective.

Memes are active forms of communication, as they allow for the articulation of intricate information in the form of interactions within an Internet audience. The dynamic nature of memes simply acknowledges that multiple actors are engaged with the memetic content. The meme creator collects various mediated works to create a composite message, using text to reinforce that message. In turn, audience members attempt to craft a collective interpretation to process that message into essential information. Both parties in this interaction are developing meaning within the medium.

One of the paradigms that effectively explains how these interactions work comes from Neil Stephenson's (1992) classic work of science-fiction *Snow Crash*. He describes the idea of a neurolinguistic virus: using language in such a way that it alters the minds of those exposed to these works. Memes force the viewer to engage with the content and information that shortcuts the normal mental processes to expose them to the digital work's underlying messaging. Stephenson extends the idea of a neurolinguistic virus by describing people's relationship to communication. He uses Sumerian language to define people as "ears with bodies attached, passive receivers of information" (pg. 394).

Any aspect of this innovative model of Internet interaction acts as an orientation to others' opinions. Each of the mediated work elements has an essential purpose in expressing thoughts and ideas engraved in the collective mindset. The loud representation of individual views is made calmer and brighter by applying mediated works that can provide clarity of vision to the blurry world of the Internet and, mostly, social media platforms. The active nature of memes referred to in the last definition of the previous chapter is counter to the stillness of other mediums online.

I am not suggesting that videos are not a composition of moving images (they are) or that there are no technological processes that move pixels on a screen (there are). The stillness I am referring to is the stillness of the mind when processing most forms of online content. Marshall McLuhan (1964) referred to the serenity of the mind when describing the two media types. Hot media (which includes most audio and video works) demands little audience participation by providing contextually-dense presentation within the mediated work. Memes would be considered a cold medium (along with speeches, conversation, and infographics) as it forces the audience to participate more in interpreting the work.

Memes are a cold medium; they force the audience to perceive the meaning behind the message. Audience members perform a perceptual analysis of the meme when they deconstruct all of its parts to come to a deeper understanding of the meme's message. This analysis can only happen when a person examines each of the memetic artifact's layers separately.

DEFINING LAYERS

Deconstructing memes requires understanding the layers that make up the meme. A layer in this sense refers to a composite for three different communication aspects that provides the skeleton for all memetic communication. There first must be a mode of interaction that allows for the placement of contextual information. This mode might be a medium of communication, a social exchange between cultural aspects, or a series of observable actions to exchange meaningful information. The term *mode* is centrally referring to the standing set of practices that one would take to engage with others.

The second component that defines a layer is contextual information added on top of the medium, social exchange, or observable actions. If the mode is the canvas of expression within the meme, the contextual information acts as the paint on top of the canvas. It provides the starting point of how one could interpret the underlying message of the meme. Modes are static presentation platforms that can be easily identified. Contextual information reflects the personal decision of the meme creator interacting with the cultural and social spirit of the community in which the meme will be placed.

The last part of any layer is simply the "instructions" for interpreting the contextual information within the mode of interaction. These instructions explain how one can read the layer. The theoretical aspects of this part will be discussed in greater detail at the end of this chapter. The presentation of this role in this chapter is not to say there is only one way to read the information presented in the meme; instead, this by-product of memetic artifacts forces those attempting to understand memes better as a starting point for explaining the complexity of these mediated works.

One of the critical aspects to note about layers is that memetic artifacts do not need to have all of the layers listed here to be considered a meme. The composition of memes is as dynamic and diverse as the meme creators that produce them. The more layers a meme has adds to the meaningful messaging's density and complexity within that meme. Scholars studying these works can provide more clarity on the intricate messaging within the meme. Those in the psychological professions might consider multiple layers of the meme as a foundation for meaningful discussion during a session.

Layers are the vital elements that make memes these compelling works that we share to make our friends laugh, use as evidence in arguments, or express who we are within society. Understanding the layers allows us to understand better who we are and how we interact in society.

CONCEPTUAL LAYER

One of the first layers to examine is a layer we could call a "proto-layer." Like a prototype, the meme is being drafted in the mind of the content creator before any work begins on a computer. This layer addresses how the meme creator translates their beliefs, values, experiences, and views of the world into memetic form.

"Conceptual layers," as we are describing them in this book, focuses on both the underlying inspiration for the meme they create and how other memes influence the creation process. Memetic content is rooted in both of these aspects.

Calling conceptual layers proto-layers allows for the deep-dive into the psychological motivations of the meme creator. Proto-layers are the starting points in the full development of a given meme. They reference back to the idea of a meme being a gene from Her's definition of the term. It is the mediated construction of a meme creator's interpretation of a singular cultural thought or social truth. If the meme creator addresses a cultural thought, they are speaking towards the community's moral, spiritual, or aesthetic standards. Social truths are often a composite of individual experiences that resonate with the larger community.

A first step in deconstructing a memetic artifact's conceptual layer is understanding how this meme fits in with the others typically used within a community. This acknowledgment recognizes the process of social learning described in the previous chapter. Meme creators see the means of effectively addressing their audience and then borrow those techniques to present a message to the community. The thing that the meme creator wants to transmit must be in a form that community members will understand as a meme and engage with it.

Interpreting the conceptual layer requires the scholar to have some sense of what the meme creator is like. A basic interpretation level could be demographic (gender, education, location, income, etc.) in nature. The individual characteristics that led to the meme's creation are often an excellent place to begin such an analysis. Psychographic analysis (the needs, wants, and desires of the individual) can present a more explicit definition of the meme's conceptual impact, if the scholar avoids misunderstanding what the meme creator was thinking when they started to create their meme.

TEXTUAL LAYER

Textual layers are the first level of analysis that has clear mediated elements within the meme. This layer is the one that the meme creator has the most control in adjusting to match the message they want to transmit to the community. Others can mutate the text of a meme in turn. These mutations need to balance providing novel information (so as not to repeat previous memes) and maintaining the accepted structure or syntax of the words used by others (to be accepted by the community as a derivative of the original context).

The medium of communication within this layer was discussed in detail in the previous chapter. Alphabetic glyphs (i.e., letters, numbers, and symbols that one could type on a standard keyboard) are placed on the meme using consistent typeface. Impact typeface tends to be the de facto text style for memes (as Times New Roman tends to be the de facto typeface for academic works). The meme aesthetic often begins with an image with words in the Impact typeface. This configuration of visual information informs the viewer that they might be looking at a meme.

The text is a narrow channel of communication that, by itself, does not make a meme. Merely labeling a picture with this popular font does not necessarily present a complex message that most people would consider a meme (nor would it fit the definitions of a meme listed in the first chapter). Words on the meme need to explain a social truth or cultural thought related to the moment in which the meme is being posted and to the rest of the layers within the meme.

Interpreting text within a meme can be a simple reading of words and comprehending their meaning. No additional work is needed. There can be further context to the words depending on the community in which the meme is being presented. The significance of different terms and phrases used by various community members is useful to denote as a reference point.

VISUAL LAYER

The other element that represents what traditionally would be considered part of any meme is the visual layer. Superimposing text on top of a graphic is often known as an **image macro style** of memes. Visual layers are not just a simple wallpaper to the textual layers. While they act as a backdrop to some aspects of the memetic content, the optical elements add additional contextual information and meaning. There are four categories of visuals that meme creators can add to get something across to the community.

Stock photography and other forms of commonly accessible graphics tend to be among the more popular visual layers added to memetic content. The optical elements in question typically have no specific meaning to any community. These visuals will have a generic interpretation among community members and no other contextual messaging within the image. Meme creators will tend to impose a memetic meaning based on how the image is used with a meme, as there is no cultural meaning that the community would consistently associate with the image. Sometimes this imposed memetic meaning will extend beyond the memetic content. Examples of visuals with imposed memetic meanings are Lazy College Senior, Royalty-Free Ukulele, Hide the Pain Harold, and Distracted Boyfriend.

Figure 5: A reenactment of the "Distracted Boyfriend" meme's visual layer. The title of the iStock version of this visual is "Jealous Girlfriend Calling Boyfriend Distracted By Other Attractive Woman stock photo." The visual itself has no deeper meaning than being a stock photo. The visual is typically used to represent the conflict between something that should be done or is available versus taking a risk or desiring something. It is a visual representation of that feeling. Source: iStock

Another category of graphics that can be used in this layer is directly adapted from **popular culture**. Those images are more likely than not to be easily identifiable to a general audience. Characters from popular works already have an established cultural meaning to the audience based on those characters' behaviors, attributes, attitudes, and other personality traits. Meme creators have the option to exaggerate those personality traits, debase the actions of the character, or have the character be a stand-in for the meme creator or audience. Symbols from popular culture works can be mutated in similar ways. The meme creator is **adapting**

and adjusting the character or symbol's cultural meaning to fit the context of the situation and the meme. Spongebob Squarepants tends to be the most famous example in this category of visuals.

The last two categories of images involve real world crossover. The first uses pictures and photographs from news organizations. Typically these visuals relate to some newsworthy event that has significance to the community. These **newsworthy events** do not directly impact the given community; instead, community members are generally aware of the story's aspects that relate to the images. Meme creators using a newsworthy image tend to **interpret the significance** of the image to the community and use the meme to reinforce that significance as part of the something that the meme is trying to communicate. One example of using a newsworthy image came from the 2021 Euro Finals in football when the Italian captain Giorgio Chiellini pulled the jersey of English player Saka. One of the memes from the image used the text "When you walk away from your laptop and forget that your headphones are still plugged in." Even the Malta Police Force used that image during a weather emergency to warn people about making weekend beach plans.

Figure 6: Malta Police Force using a newsworthy visual layer in the meme as an overexaggaration to "pull back" the plans for the weekend. The image from the Euro Final is a significant visual as it appears to reinforce the concept of "pulling back" the weekend plans of those that live in Malta. Source: Malta Police Force's Facebook page

Finally, **other real-world images** that are not directly related to popular culture works or newsworthy events. These images tend to resonate with community members to the point of reflecting the spirit of the community. This category's crucial component is that these images reflect a **performance** (whether that is a real performance observed by the community or an imagined one that suits some communal purpose). NBC's (2020) *Saturday Night Live* skit "Uncle Meme" starring John Mulaney is a fair example of this accidental virality of this category of images.

COMPOSITIONAL LAYER

The last layer that the meme creator contributes is directly related to how they put it together. The compositional layer examines what techniques were used in crafting the meme. It is fair to acknowledge that sites like MemeGenerator.net, Imgflip, or Canva make it easy to create a meme. Analyzing this aspect of the meme looks for the inspiration behind how the previously listed layers are intentionally put together. Understanding this point adds an additional layer of meaning to the meme.

Gaining meaning from this layer requires a baseline deconstruction of the meme. The meme itself is a medium of communication (as defined in the previous chapter) and becomes part of the messaging of the something being transmitted by the meme creator. A baseline deconstruction can be first addressed by determining if the meme uses a memetic template to craft the message. Memetic templates are essentially the IKEA directions of building a meme. They are abstract as there is no dominant language to tell the meme creator how to make the meme. Sometimes, both show precisely where to play the various parts to craft the end-product. Finally, both can be adapted regardless of what community a person comes from or what language they speak. Many of the previous paragraph's sites use memetic templates as a starting point to craft a meme. Most of these templates have a recognized name that allows them to be categorized by others.

Once a meme creator has mastered the meme's primary form that the memetic template teaches, they can use other tools to craft their work. Some of the more popular tools to create memes are GIMP, Pixlr, and Vectr, as these options are mostly free (if not completely free) to use. Those trained in Adobe Illustrator (or any other professional graphic design software) would find it an easy tool to produce memes. Because these works typically do not follow the memetic template formulas, they would not be easy to categorize or assess based on production alone.

CULTURAL LAYER

Memes are more than the mediated elements that are placed together to present a message. These creative works tap into the books, movies, television shows, games, graphic novels, and other imaginative displays that speak to the human condition and state of society. Meme creators pick the components from those creative works that best connect with the something they are trying to express and add those components to the meme's cultural layer. These elements require the audience to have the right cultural capital to decode their meaning. When talking about memetic content, cultural capital generally refers to the knowledge of a community member based on how they were socialized (embodied cultural capital). What a community member owns (objectified cultural capital) and their professional qualifications or academic credentials (institutionalized cultural capital) play a limited role or no role at all in understanding the cultural layer of a meme (Bourdieu, 1999).

Effective presentations of the cultural layer depend on the community's collective embodied cultural capital being related to the community's shared social experiences that have deeper meaningful connections to social truths and/or cultural norms of the community. Cultural content depends on the community members having a similar series of interpretations of what the various characters or symbols mean to the community. If this is not the case, the memes will fail to connect with the community at large.

Clear interpretations of a meme's cultural layer depend on understanding the significance of the characters or symbol to the community. Scholars should recognize if the community seems to the passionate guardian of popular culture knowledge, analytic recorders of fan culture, quiet champions of creative works, engagers with the rest of the world through mediated references, or a hybrid of all of the above depending on the situation (Tilton, 2016). Typically, this understanding level comes from an in-depth reading of the community members' other postings on that social media platform.

Figure 7: An example of the addition of a textual layer ("serious heart hands") to a visual layer. The composition of this meme is an animated gif. Overall, this meme is a remix of the original context. The original version was performed by Safiya Nygaard on her YouTube channel, which is part of the cultural layer of the meme. Source: Dr. Ryan Kelly #OneTrueGif

PERFORMATIVE LAYER

All of the layers previously defined in this chapter work well for the two-dimensional spaces that most memes take up. As memes migrate from the online expanses to real-world interactions, meme creators become architects of movements, interactions, and symbols that will form a collective ritual for a given community (Rothenbuhler & Coman, 2005). The popularity of these real-world performances is driven by communal sharing of these practices and the ease of performing the collective actions (Mina, 2019). In this layer of the meme, community members will actively engage with the meme by adopting the meme's actions and presenting those actions in real world situations.

Deconstructing this layer of the meme means understanding that this layer is one of the first ones where the audience and the community must be actively engaged with the memetic content for the meme to spread. The previous layers directly relate to the construction of the meme. Performative layers are built as a series of actions that the community can observe and recreate instead of merely adding content or ideas to the layer. The standing set of practices within the layer is based on a form of media literacy, where the audience is aware they are allowed to participate in the meme's performance. An excellent example of this level of audience awareness would be the "Ice Bucket Challenge."

Scholars and psychological professionals contextualizing any memetic performance need to account for cultural influences within the meme. Other creative performances influence all performers of the meme (and the meme creator, as well) in what actions to take when reenacting the elements of the meme. These influences can range from waiting to imitate celebrities in the meme, incorporating other works of popular culture, adding local references to the meme, or even allowing the performers to highlight their talents and voice within the memetic performance. Those attempting to deconstruct the memetic artifact need to recognize the differences between this performance and the meme's original context.

One additional area to consider when interpreting the meme from the vantage point of the performance layer is that the social media platform where the meme is posted acts as the stage or theater for the performance. Sometimes the interaction between the audience and the performers is more critical to contextualize than the performance alone. As memes are an active mode of communication, the audience plays a role in interpreting the message and adding to the overall understanding of what the meme represents.

CONTEXTUAL LAYER

A necessary and straightforward layer to discuss in the analysis of a meme is how the community uses it as part of social interactions. It is the point that the content becomes a way for the community members to express themselves in the "lingua franca" that connects the majority of modern online populations and allows the memetic content to go beyond the confines of an individual mode of expression (Milner, 2018). The questions to address if one were to describe this layer to others (either in the process of analyzing the meme or for the purpose of using memes in a therapeutic session) are:

1. How is the meme being used by community members?

2. What about this meme makes it a popular one among the community?

3. What is the rationale for using this meme?

4. Who does this meme speak for?

5. Who does this meme speak to?

6. Why should community members use this meme as a form of expression?

These questions speak to the social-psychological nature of memetic communication and how community members express themselves to others. A spin-off of answering these inquiries is that the person studying the meme will understand better the social norms that allow a person to use a given meme.

All analyses of this layer of the meme depend on a clear description of the social exchanges based on the related meme. The only way a person can offer a narrative that matches the community's reality is by having a keen understanding of how the group defines itself. These examples must clearly show behavioral patterns that afford some insights into the social mindset of the community. Anthropologists and sociologists would call these examples the artifacts of the community.

A second-level analysis requires defining how community members would interpret their use of those selected artifacts. This point of reflection gets to the beliefs and values of community members. Revealing these aspects of the community is much more difficult and time-consuming but can allow for a more in-depth insight into that community's social bonds. The community's spirit is crystallized in the individual expression and judgment provided by examining this layer of the meme.

Combining the answers to the six questions listed above with the two levels of analyses described in this section allows for a meaningful accounting of how people actually engage with one another. Done well, a precise explanation of the layer will show how these interactions influence community members' perceptions of the world. Injecting this information into the meme's description explains the complexity of these modes of interaction.

RHETORICAL LAYER

Because memes are a form of complex communication, another avenue to examine is how memes mimic communication situations. Specifically, memes are more than the interactions between the meme's poster or creator and the community. There is an entire rhetorical situation that defines the scope of the meme. The previous layers began to address the meme's messaging as a form of text that can be studied (and this point will be discussed in the last part of this chapter). Three additional elements worth noting are the purpose of presenting such a work, the setting that is facilitating such a work, and how the occasion influences the perception of the work at the time it was posted.

Purpose should be defined for this layer of analysis as the reasoning that the meme creator had for crafting the memetic artifact for their audience. This definition sounds similar to a couple of the points raised by earlier sections in this chapter. The difference is that this idea forces the person studying the meme first to consider that the meme creator is attempting to communicate with an audience instead of a given community. Communities have active levels of engagement between community members. Audiences are a collective respondent that the meme creator essentially has to imagine they are talking to when creating their meme.

Setting means addressing how the platform facilitates interactions between the meme creator and the audience. Acknowledging this point focuses on how the meme creator expects to get feedback from the community and its members. Another aspect of this concept is thinking about how the platform privileges certain content, messaging, and performances while filtering out other communication attempts. Identifying what is privileged and what will be filtered addresses the role the setting plays with this layer.

Discussing occasion means taking into account all of the cultural and social influences that lead to crafting the meme and being posted on a social network. A memetic artifact does not exist in a culture-less vacuum. The community, poster, and meme creator are all influenced by culture for the reasons listed earlier in this book. Those cultural influences will impact how the meme creator crafts the meme, how the poster will support the posting of that meme, and how the community will interpret that meme. The reason for discussing occasion rather than the meme's context is that we should appreciate what is happening the moment the meme is shared with the rest of the community. The meme acts as a "snapshot of the community's reality" the moment the meme creator hits the send button.

META-ANALYTICAL LAYER

The final layer considered here is the 40,000-foot vantage point of the meme's social and cultural role. This type of analysis is a meta-analytical view of the various relationships and interactions that come along with exhibiting a meme on a social network. All of the previous layers depended on:

1. Understanding the meme creator's mindset and process when creating the meme,

2. Having clarity on the poster's status within the community and their relationship with other community members,

3. Describing how the community sees itself,

4. Explaining how community members generally feel that they connect with the rest of the community,

5. Addressing the more significant cultural and social issues that would impact the creation and reading of a meme, or

6. A combination of those five concepts.

Meta-analytical views of a meme examine how a "dispassionate layperson" would describe all of the meme layers working together to present a cohesive message. The main question addressed in this layer is, "how would a community member describe the meme to an outsider?"

A deconstruction of this layer means describing the observable actions related to this memetic artifact that the exchange of meaningful information can be clearly understood by anybody reading the description. Any description of this nature must use short, clear, and concise language to promote clarity of tone and idea. A reasonable approach for crafting this description is writing it so that an eighth-grader could easily understand what is happening.

Defining the contextual information within the layer is intentionally broad. Only observable social interactions from the vantage point of an outsider would be considered part of this layer. It is fair for the outsider to offer a loose interpretation of those actions based on a comprehensive set of standards that reflect the cultural and social norms.

The last element to consider when analyzing this layer is how a meme explains the complexity of social interactions within a given community. Specifically, the dispassionate layperson described earlier would need to clearly explain all of the rituals and actions related to the posting of a meme. Is there an expectation of feedback from the community? Is another meme used to reply to a meme? What is the indication that the community successfully understands the meme?

THE POWER OF LAYERS WITHIN A MEME

Let's look at a scenario of how these layers work together. For example, Sam wants to create a new meme. He looks out his window and sees the sun and thinks, "if I take a picture of me pretending to hold the sun, the caption 'Feel the Burn' would work with it." This thinking process is Sam applying the first layer by creating the conceptual layer for the meme.

Figure 8.a: Sam working on his meme by developing the concept (Holly McCoy)

Sam gets one of his friends to take a picture where he is under the sun with arms stretched out, and it looks like his hands are holding the sun. He uses the hypothetical site "MemeCreate' to add the caption on the image "Feel the Burn" in Impact typeface (which is the textual layer of the meme) on top of the photo that his friend just took (which is the visual layer of the meme). As Sam is not a stock photography model, a fictional character from a popular culture work, or newsworthy himself, it is his performance of the action that is worth noting.

Figure 8.b: Sam is adding text on the graphic interface to start designing his meme. (Holly McCoy)

Figure 8.c: Sam is adding the photo that his friend took his meme, becoming the visual layer of the meme. (Holly McCoy)

Now, MemeCreate limits where the text can be placed on the image and adds its logo to its bottom. Both of those elements make up the compositional layer of the meme. It is a very basic meme that was put together relatively quickly. This one image represents an original context in Shifman's Four Phases of Memetic Works.

Figure 8.d: MemeCreate is finalizing the design on its website by adding the logo of the site of the bottom. This piece of information allows a person that the meme was crafting using the MemeCreate template system, which is part of the compositional layer. (Holly McCoy)

Let us say, for the sake of argument, that Sam's meme becomes popular in his group. One of Sam's friends, Pat, decides to remix the original meme. Their group likes anime. Pat takes an image from Dragonball Z where Goku is holding a fireball above his head. Pat decides to photoshop clothes on Goku that look like the ones Sam was wearing in the original content. Pat has remixed the original context by adding a cultural layer on top of that first meme. The meme is now infused with the cultural capital associated with Dragonball Z, aspects of anime, and what Sam, Pat, and their friends feel about those reference points. Goku is a powerful character within the show and reinforces the powerfulness of the meme.

Sam's friends (in the words of Shifman) have used the meme

so much in their online interactions that they decided to recreate the meme. They go out and replicate the pose and the image. This recreation adds another layer on top of the final meme they created. It would no longer have the cultural layer from the previous paragraph (unless one of their friends was Goku and they were in the image) but gains a performative layer as his friends mimicked the original performance for this new meme.

Figure 8.e: Two of Sam's friends performing the original meme to mimic its original context. (Holly McCoy)

We now should look at how Sam and his friends use new versions of this meme. Jo, another friend, says something stupid. Pat calls them out on their dumb statement. Sam uses his original "Feel the Burn" meme to reinforce that Pat just burned Jo. This meme's contextual layer is now applied to the meme as it is used as a reaction. This interaction also reveals the rhetorical layer of the meme. Sam's purpose for creating this meme was a lighthearted way to make fun of his friends when they said dumb things online. The setting makes the original context more meaningful as it is Sam in the meme, and his friends all know who he is. If the meme became hypermemetic, meaning another community used Sam's original meme, it would be meaningful in a different way.

Figure 8.f: Two of Sam's friends using Sam's meme contextually in an online conversation. (Holly McCoy)

As the omnipresent narrator in this example, I would look at the entire scenario and say that the group uses this meme to point out funny statements that other group members make from time-to-time. If the memes were overused against Jo, it could be considered a spiteful reaction to reinforce Jo's lower group status (especially if Sam created this meme to pick on Jo). This read of the social situation is the meme's meta-analytical layer.

This scenario, like this chapter, focused on the interplay between the different layers of a meme to understand why this particular mediated work is an active mode of communication. Other Internet content mirrors traditional media as it relates to its audience. Most of the time, the work is a performance in which the community is a passive audience that consumes the work. The audience might be using mobile devices to receive such content, but they are most likely sitting down and listening/reading/watching the performance with limited reactions to the work. Using Chi and Wylie's (2014) ICAP Framework (Interactive, Constructive, Active, and Passive audience models), memetic communication seems to move away from the passive audience model to a more constructive or interactive audience model. The community members are developing newer memes to respond to others' comments and memes.

Memes are designed to engage with the community to get some form of reaction. These reactions can be lighthearted and joking or inspire more serious logical and ethical discourse about an important issue. The way the audience reads these memes begin with their construction. Meme creators that can effectively weave layers together to craft a compelling piece of rhetorical work will find that the community is more likely to listen to them and what they have to say. The second part of this engagement comes from the way the community and audience read the meme itself.

STUART HALL & THE READING OF LAYERS

One of the theorists whose work can constructively help with reading memes is Stuart Hall. Hall's work in communication was considered groundbreaking in the 1970s for his approach to critique of mass media's cultural influence. He was one of the first scholars to address the production of mediated work in a way that incorporated how audiences would interpret those pieces of content. The dissemination of mass media became as scholarly accessible as analyzing a book. We need to look at Stuart Hall's analysis of encoding and decoding communication processes to understand how to read the various layers, each of which we can engage with using Hall's model of reading the media.

Hall's (2001) *Encoding/Decoding* gives a solid framework for discussing the relationship between content creators and their audience and addressing how the content flows from those creators to the audience. Through any communication channel, the encoding process depends on the content creator finding the right symbols that the audience will recognize, allowing the creator's message to be clearly understood. Decoding content requires the audience to interpret the creator's central idea by understanding the intent behind each of the symbols used in the message and the significance of their placement within the medium of communication.

This decoding process is central to how an audience member reads the content. Hall theorized three different ways to read mediated works. A straightforward beginning to Hall's coding model is that the audience members use the **dominant-hegemonic code** to interpret the content's central message. This interpretation means that the audience member decodes the message within the mediated work and reads the content the way the creator meant it to be read. **Hegemonic** refers to a view of the world that is promoted by influential figures within society. These views essentially dominate most forms of social and mediated discourse.

A second code used to read mediated works is the **oppositional code**. This type of code means that the person receiving the message understands the communicator's intended message yet completely rejects the premise of the content. The person receiving the message changes the concept behind the content to add their own meaning to the content. The receiver's changes directly oppose the dominant thinking on the subject being discussed in the content. In addition, the receiver interprets the message oppositely from the sender's intent. It is often because the content or messaging is not relatable to the receiver, the structure does not reflect their society, it is controversial, or they simply disagree, so they do not understand it in the same sense. One example of oppositional reading is when a conspiracy theorist receives a government report about a UFO sighting, 9/11, or vaccines. The receiver believes that the government is lying to them and, therefore, the story is just a fabrication of what "really happened."

The final code that an audience member can use to read the media is a **negotiated code**. Using this code will accept and reject elements within the content based on their experiences, beliefs, and values. This coding allows the audience to recognize the dominant message that the creator is attempting to send but resists the underlying message to modify it based on those previously listed internal factors.

Hall's work is compelling when applied to memetic communication. Each layer allows for a different type of contextual information encoded within the meme. Meme creators can apply a dominant-hegemonic, oppositional, or negotiated position to a given layer when crafting the meme. Community members are then granted additional decoding opportunities when examining the meme. A person could choose to apply an oppositional view to the textual layer, negotiated reading of the cultural layer, and a dominant-hegemonic reading of the visuals. The complexity of the memetic artifact is the foundation for a rich reading of the mediated work.

THE THERAPEUTIC ANGLE

Approaching a therapeutic session with the understanding that memes are a composition of layers that promote active communication practices gives the therapist some different tools to address underlying concerns and issues. These tools go beyond the casual observations about memes. Those that understand the power of these memetic layers a chance to use memetic content as part of a therapeutic session.

A model of beginning such a conversation is what I like to call the "jigsaw puzzle" paradigm. The world is filled with nearly unlimited creative works that could act as the pieces to complete the jigsaw puzzle, or in this case, the finished meme. Start by asking the creator, "what inspired the selection of those different parts of meme when you crafted the meme?" The variation of this question for someone that posts memes could be, "what is your favorite element of this meme and why?" Both of these questions can garner insight into how the client connects with popular culture. Clients are more apt to discuss cultural symbols that resonate with them when using this prompt. Great follow-up questions can prompt discussion of the beliefs and values that the client attaches to these cultural symbols.

A deeper dive depends on the cultural competency level that the counselor conducting the conversation has concerning the meme being discussed. This process is a multiple-session arc, as it may take time to research the cultural symbols and popular culture content referenced with the meme. This conversation requires an open dialogue and a willingness to learn about the culture sincerely.

Works Cited

Bourdieu, P. (1999). Cultural Reproduction and Social Reproduction. *Modernity: Cultural Modernity, 2, 351.*

Chi, M. T., & Wylie, R. (2014). The ICAP Framework: Linking cognitive engagement to active learning outcomes. *Educational Psychologist*, 49(4), 219-243.

Hall, S. (2001). Encoding/decoding. In M. G. Durham & D. Kellner (Eds.), *Media and Cultural Studies: Keyworks (pp. 163–173). Blackwell Publishers.*

McLuhan, M. (1964). *Understanding Media: The extensions of man.* McGraw Hill.

Mina, A. X. (2019). *Memes to Movements: How the world's most viral media is changing social protest and power.* Beacon Press.

NBC. (2020, February 29). John Mulaney. *Saturday Night Live.* episode, New York City, NY.

Rothenbuhler, E. W., & Coman, M. (Eds.). (2005). *Media Anthropology. Sage Publications.*

Stephenson, N. (1992). Snow Crash. Bantam Books.

Tilton, S. (2016). *The Four Temperaments of Fandom.* Retrieved December 10, 2020 from: https://www.academia.edu/26449531/The_Four_Temperaments_of_Fandom

CHAPTER 3: THE MEMETIC STRUCTURES OF COMMUNITIES AND COLLECTIVES

Another point that shows the complexity of memes is how they spread so quickly to others. The construction of this mediated work is merely the first part of what makes a meme a compelling piece of content worth our scholarly focus. The extension of the last definition of the first chapter means that we need to discuss why memes are the perfect vessels for transmitting meaningful messages throughout a social network. They are more than passive displays of cultural and social norms wrapped up in a rhetorical structure that allows for massive engagement. In addition to that, memes are an effective mode of engagement as social networks promote this type of content throughout the system with a limited amount of structural resistance.

Social networks connect a wide variety of actors, organizations, locations, systems, and technologies under one standard superstructure (McLean, 2016). **Actors** are any element within the network that can present a position to the social network, an **organization** is a collaboration of actors, a **location** is the centralized arena in which interactions happen, a **system** is how actors connect, and **technologies** are the tools that best facilitate that connection. These sociological constructions have their roots in real-world interactions denoted by anthropologists in the 1950s.

The work of J.A. Barnes in the late 1950s and Mark Granovetter in the 1970s lead to the discovery that the communities we associate with are not a random set of relationships, but rather an observable set of connections that we are most comfortable with and which forms our circle of trust (strong-ties) that also contain a series of informal interactions with others in a given community that includes the foundations of most of the relationships we have within that given community (weak-ties), and a level of recognition that others exist within our community without direct interactions with them (invisible-ties) to strengthen the community (Granovetter, 2005). Understanding these ties within a social network permits those studying them to model the interactions that occur and grant a level of clarity on how social networks will generally react to internal and external stimuli.

These sociological constructions allow for transformative exchanges that go beyond the boundaries traditionally established by such a social structure. Online social networks have some of the benefits of a mass communication system as they allow for a limited broadcasting capability. People use the feeds or timelines as a proxy for communicating with the larger community. Depending on the privacy settings one has when they post, a single piece of content can be shared outside of the social network.

The power of a single piece of content comes from the idea that memes can help pull people from the general public towards a given social network, so much so that they might become part of it. Memes often highlight the social network norms in a form that can pique outsiders' interest and encourage engagement with that community. There are multiple interconnections and chain reactions that the meme can facilitate to increase the range and membership of a given social network. Exposure to new ideas, philosophies, social arrangements, and communication practices happens due to a complex piece of mediated work positively connecting with the internal motivations of the uninitiated.

Memes help maintain the connection people have with one another within the social network. Memes become a de facto language of the social network that reinforces community members' shared social experiences and codifies those experiences into a mediated form that others can share. This codification begins in the smallest possible groupings of a social network, which are dyads and triads.

DYADS, TRIADS, AND COHESIVE SUBGROUPS

All social networks are built on relationships. All social interactions start with just two people forming a relationship. **Relationships** will be contextually defined as a working alliance between two actors that share some commonalities, which form the foundation of their connection. Social networks represent relationships through the development of dyads. **Dyads** are the smallest units that exchange information and interactions within a social network while sharing common attributes. The concerns surrounding simple dyads are that an individual who only has dyadic relationships is less likely to maintain some connection to a larger community, as those relationships lack the emotional complexity that people need to connect with others in society (Brass & Borgatti, 2019).

A more complex relationship that promotes emotional health is the triad. **Triads** are where social structures start to form within a network based on the ties between three actors within the system. These triads are better equipped to navigate the "webs of significance" (Geertz, 1973) crafted by culture's influence on members. This social unit can simplify the complicated and overwhelming nature of cultural content by reflecting on what that cultural content means to the social unit members. A triadic analysis of culture provides a level of richness that is often lacking in dyadic analysis. Triadic analyses also allow for emotional stability. An example of how traids allows for emotional stability can be show when conflict happens. Dyads are two people arguing. Traids still have two people arguing, but the traids are more likely to have a third person to act as a moderator between the two conflicting parties (Hill & McGrath, 2008). These discussions about culture will be less likely to devolve into holding positions on the opposite side of the intellectual spectrum, giving the participants of such meetings ways to defuse tension in dialogue before things boil over (Maya-Jariego, Letina, & Tinoco, 2020).

Enough triads with "a sense of shared identity" will form a **cohesive subgroup** around that identity, and develop standard communication practices that promote unity between the various triads. One of the subgroup's major traits that enable cohesiveness among the members is reachability, allowing weak-tie connections to spread information quickly throughout the social network. As McLean (2014, 28) notes, "Gossip probably spreads through weak ties rather than strong ones; if it didn't, the damage to people's reputations would not spread beyond their local network neighborhoods." The rapid spread of misinformation is another example of the strength of weak-tie connections, as shown during the "infodemic" of the last two Presidential elections and the COVID-19 pandemic (Barberá, 2018; Min & Wohn, 2020; Shrivastava et al., 2020). McLean denotes the two other traits that increase cohesiveness are the hierarchical order of members among the network (the "nanocelebrities" within the group (Tilton, 2011) maintaining the interest of people within the social network) and the centrality of certain people within the social network (how well-connected some of the members are within the social network).

These three social units are influenced by memetic communication in different ways. Dyadic relationships use memetic communication as a form of social shorthand to simplify communication. A practical example to show how this shorthand works is a gif war. **Gif wars** happen when a person posts a gif and is almost immediately responded to by another gif (Jones, 2018). Beyond the fact that this event centers around the actions, reactions, and interactions of people online, gif wars depend on maintaining a cohesive narrative between the memes. This chain reaction game only works if the parties mostly agree on the meaning behind the gifs and see the common elements between two chronologically connected memes.

Triadic relationships use memes as a form of consensus agreement between the three actors in the social unit. Consensus is not necessarily explicit when memes are used within triads; rather, there is an underlying shared social experience that drives the meaning of these memes when presented in the context of a triadic dialogue.

Finally, cohesive subgroups express social norms within the memes. Symbols within memes allow the group to orient itself around the meaning of the meme's signs and its various layers. The subgroup's reachability gives memes the direct connection to its members through a centrally connected person who can express those important ideals to the rest of the group.

Acknowledging these social units is not designed to force a person to craft models of a given social network or even build a paradigm of interactions within the social network; instead, this knowledge is crucial in explaining memes' power online. The superstructures depicted in this model help clarify two of the major social networks that drive memetic communication: communities and collectives.

DEFINING COMMUNITIES

As defined by Tönnies (2017), **communities** develop cultural interactions among their members as a means of maintaining cohesion within this subgroup. These cultural interactions are more likely to be informal to strengthen the weak-tie relationships within this social unit. We can think of these everyday interactions as small talk or simple gestures of acknowledging others in the real world. Online, these rituals can be commenting on posts or liking messages.

There is an organic division of labor within this social unit that allows for the maintenance of community members' enjoyment. Community members within an online social network will tend to gravitate toward the aspects of communal interactions that have the most success or offer the highest reward. These actions will help perform two of the vital activities that maintain a cohesive subgroup. Most of the various tasks within an online social network involve spreading content and information, which increases the community's reachability factor. Those who perform more of these tasks successfully will improve their hierarchical standing.

Maintaining this level of enjoyment among community members allows them to feel a kinship among others within the community in the form of a virtual neighborhood. Most of the emotional labor of maintaining this kinship falls on the moderators of the various groups, pages, and sites that comprise the social units (Dosono & Semaan, 2019). Still, the community members enable dialogues about the issues that face the community and the topics that members are addressing. These dialogues are often in the memes and other postings by community opinion leaders and influencers.

The role of a community opinion leader or influencer defaults to those who have been in the community the longest or the person with the most wisdom about a given situation that the organization or its members are facing. Most of the time, acknowledging who is an opinion leader within a social network is based on when community members adopt a person's recommendations within the community. **Opinion leaders** will have some level of experience and expertise in a given situation and understand the best means of communicating that knowledge and wisdom to the rest of the community. **Influencers** are those within the social unit who share a considerable amount of personal resources to help the community. Typically, we associate influencers with how they craft their message to the community instead of the embedded wisdom within those messages.

One of the most effective means that opinion leaders and influencers connect with the rest of the community is through memetic communication. Communal memes can express cultural capital, institutional knowledge, and the development of community resources. Institutional knowledge spread through a meme is functionally no different than communicating propaganda or slogans in the real world. All three appeal to the audience through unique content and pleasing aesthetics. Memes can present best practices for communal interactions to maintain the community's cohesiveness. These practices are different from what would be found in a collective.

DEFINING COLLECTIVES

Unlike communities, collectives depend on a collection of common characteristics to define a social unit's boundaries. McLean (2016) gave the term a broad stroke to refer to any object within a social network that could be grouped and studied collectively. Memes can exist as a collective as easily as a group of people on a social network. The three critical parts of a collective form a lovely rhyming trio:

Nodes are the focal points of any given collective. In the online social network realm of collectives, nodes are represented by two separate yet equally important concepts: the people within the social network and the bots that allow automated interactions and conversations within the social network. Both nodes are vital for the health of the social network. Real humans are needed to keep the collective engaged with important topics, issues, and events beyond the online social network's boundaries and into the real world. Bots can report other nodes' actions within the collective, information and knowledge from the real world, or even significant data that needs monitoring.

Roads are the connections made between actors/nodes within the collective. A model or drawing of the roads within a social network will show how the different nodes interact with one another. Formal social network analysis calls these connections the network's edges, as they start to mark the social network's boundaries. For online social networks, pages and groups tend to be the more obvious representations of roads, as membership is visible to others via profile links and other public markers. Another road is a hashtag that denotes special events, highlights a topic, or presents sides to an issue.

The last part of a collective is the **load**, which refers to the content that nodes add to the road. It is this part of the collective that memes fit into this discussion. Thinking of memes as part of the load within a collective means that those researching this form of communication can apply basic analytical techniques to group those works and how actors distribute them via the network. One of the elements that aids with the transmission of content are the technologies that actors use to craft the content. These technologies are both the physical hardware tools that people can use to take analog experiences and convert them into a digital platform and the software that people and bots use as their window and voice into the world's online social networks.

Viewing social networks as collectives perform two crucial tasks that communities cannot do. The most pressing task related to this book is helping scholars analyze memes in a meaningful way. Collectives sorts memes into categories based on how they are used within specific arenas of engagement online. There are social and cultural cues that inform posters when and where to use certain memes based on feedback from the social network. cues taken from how well the meme fits into a specific context.

The last task is critical because framing the social networks as collectives helps move the conservation away from the nebulous nature of interactions within social networks toward defining social norms of the network. It focuses on addressing the common characteristics that maintain the cohesive connections between members. The acknowledgment of those common characteristics allows us to address the two types of Internets that drive memetic communication.

THE INTERNET AND INTERNET OF MEMES

The Internet is an invisible part of everyday social interactions in most parts of the world. People traditionally do not think about it unless it is down. It acts as our lifeline to others and how we navigate the rest of society. While there are significant populations today that do not have reliable Internet access (Sicheri, 2019), they can travel with some comfort to connect to this powerful social tool more often than not. Addressing the Internet is vital to explain how memes influence society. This analysis means addressing the two types of Internets that people come across every day.

The (capital I) **Internet**, for cultural discussions, is a superstructure that allows for the distribution of files and folders between computers. It is easy to overlook that there are programs that control every aspect of the online experience as we have almost reached the point of instantaneous access to Internet content. The pathways in the virtual realm are nearly invisible to the average user. It would be unusual to think about the file structure of their favorite website. Instead, they would use the search bar or click on a link shared by one of their friends to get the content they were looking for. This seamless experience is a by-product of decades of technological development to democratize online communication and the services one could use in this space. It is this experience that has to lead to the evolution of the second internet.

The (lowercase i) **internet**, for cultural discussions, is the social co-construction that allows for communities and societies to transmit cultural artifacts. For lack of better language, it is an imagined place that the writer William Gibson in his best-selling book Neuromancer (1988) described as "a consensual hallucination experienced daily by billions of legitimate operators" (pg. 5). This fabricated shared social experience among the internet users means that people are crafting their social realities from the starting point of the nothingness of the black mirror that they are staring at before their devices power up for use. A blank canvas allows internet users to redefine themselves in the space and use this arena of discourse to address the issues, interests, and events that strike their fancy based on their behaviors and values.

McLean (2016) addresses the intersection of Internets when discussing social behaviors and information within social networks. He attempts to put some practical limits on connecting the two to avoid taking an overly broad view. McLean's analysis is coming for a point of reasonable reflection. We will attempt to untangle and reconnect these concepts throughout the book to explain the psychological benefit of analyzing memes and discussing memes as a powerful agent within Internet culture. Internet (with a capital I) is the default term that will be used for the rest of the book, with the internet (with a lowercase i) being used to specifically address cultural issues independent of a network superstructure (i.e., the mass consensual hallucination that we share).

It is essential to approach these concepts, as they directly impact memes' ability to spread throughout a social network. Collectives act closer to the Internet model since both tend to focus on social networks' structural components. On the other hand, communities are more in-line with the internet model because both depend on social interactions to define the social network's nature. Both communities and collectives are at the heart of the memetic structure, directing these mediated works' movements between members. Any of these memetic structures' power to move memes between members depends on the factors that define a thriving social network (Tilton, 2020).

CRITICAL MASS OF USERS

Four key factors impact users' ability within social networks to spread memes far and wide. Any content that reaches significantly beyond a given social network happens first when that social network has a critical mass of users actively engaging with one another regularly. A social network has a **critical mass of users** occurs when:

1. A reasonable majority of those people who use the platform get to the point that they feel confident to use the platform regularly (Al-Taie & Kadry, 2017)

2. When an individual member within the social network is more likely to connect with more than one acquaintance at a given time within the social unit to form a giant cluster of connections within their social network (Westland, 2009)

3. Those giant clusters have enough resources and actors to pursue most tasks since there is a minimum cost for performing that task and a benefit for completing that task to the cluster (Crossley & Ibrahim, 2012) and

4. There are enough "key players" within the social network to influence users' decisions, attract new members to the social network, and help the social network focus on a given task (Liu, 2020)

It makes virtually no sense to take the time and effort to develop a presence on a given social media platform if there aren't enough people to maintain that person's interest on that site. This idea of a critical mass means that users within a giant cluster are the bridge that moves memes away from the social network in which they were developed towards other social units. There are people who act as superspreaders among giant clusters through their connections to multiple different social networks. **Superspreaders** tend to share common characteristics between two or more social networks that help memes pass from one social network to another. Most of the time, a memetic artifact needs very little modification to be understood between social networks.

When memes move away from the giant cluster in which they were developed, the meme's underlying messages and context are made simpler due to the layers' flattening (Reese, 2010). Significant elements for one cluster are unlikely to be understood by an outside group. Memes do have the potential to be "lost in translation" when referencing experiences and cultural capital that a select few people would have.

When thinking about critical masses within social networks, cohesion elements can be fundamentally different between critical masses. Cultural capital tends to be specialized based on the cultural touchstones that the actors within a critical mass have been exposed to in the course of their lives. Not all critical masses will have the same shared social experiences, which bring us to the second key factor that drives memetic communication across the Internet.

DIVERSITY OF EXPERIENCES

Social networks need to have a diversity of experiences and opinions that are shared reasonably with the members in the social network. For a social network to have **a diversity of experience and opinions**, groupings must account for multiple rational discourse positions that open up members' understanding of a stated topic, issue, point of interest, or event. Rational discourse is an integral part of this factor as any position being expressed must survive being exposed to strict scrutiny by others. A member's position that falls apart once somebody questions the validity of sourcing or the rhetorical construction doesn't reflect a rational discourse.

This understanding of rational discourse does not mean that irrational conversations and memes die on the vine. A casual observer of the Internet can point to many examples in which a provable false claim or overly emotional media work is easily spread throughout a social network in memetic content. These problematic works are amplified due to some giant clusters being echo chambers. **Echo chambers** evolve when like-minded individuals who share similar ideologies repeat the same political, cultural, and social positions about subjects in the public sphere and essentially become the polarized outliers in public discourse and debate (Balsamo et al., 2019). Memes that come from echo chambers lose more contextual and rhetorical layers of meaning, as the echo chamber's cultural capital and shared social experiences are fundamentally different from the rest of the general public. The echo chamber's socialization is more specialized and fragmented than the average person's media consumption habits (Boulianne, Koc-Michalska, & Bimber, 2020).

People studying memes should find in a platform that has a diversity of experiences and opinions that multiple positions are expressed about important community subjects. Expressions of those positions aren't necessarily going to be civil but should feel like they allow for some form of debate. The critical takeaway from seeing those exchanges is that there is a free marketplace of ideas within the platform. The final result of a genuinely free marketplace of ideas is that the truthful presentations of reality will find some form of success on the forum. Simultaneously, false representations should be buried underneath the noise on the site (Schroeder, 2020).

A final point to know about the diversity factor within social networks is that a diversity of expression allows for novel inter-pretations and presentations of memetic artifacts. These creative twists on older memetic content give more life to any meme within the network and exhibit a different vantage point of the subject matter being expressed within the meme. These novel presenta-tions of community subjects within the meme lead to the third key factor in social network users' ability to transmit memes beyond a single social network effectively.

THOUGHTFUL ENGAGEMENTS

The third factor related to the effectiveness of social network users transmitting memetic content is when those users have thoughtful engagements. It is fair to define **thoughtful engagements** as those interactions in a social network where all actors are aware of others' internal states and can change their behaviors and communication practices to best address everyone's mental, emo-tional, physical, social, or psychological well-being (Kowert, 2020). Meaningful interactions are connected to thoughtful engagements as they are both based on "reading the room." One of the disad-vantages of an online social network is the inability to express non-verbal modes of communication. Facial expressions, body language, and movements are reduced to textual and two-dimensional pieces of information. Memes can add the missing context in most interactions due to the meme's complexity of messaging.

Meaningful interactions and thoughtful engagements help build connections and social norms within a social network by increasing the interactivity among members. **Interactivity** happens when suitable communication technologies allow community members to connect through smooth and secure interactions to exchange information. Community and collective members use interactive practices to process that information to turn it into knowledge about their community. As with the diversity of experiences and opinions, this process will not happen within the system regularly. It happens enough that it feels like community dialogues are happening on the site (Ross, 2018).

UNDERLYING VALUE OF INFORMATION AND KNOWLEDGE

The final factor that determines the effectiveness of members of a memetic structure to transmit these artifacts in a given social unit is the underlying value that the members place on the information and knowledge being exchanged within the network. **Underlying value** will vary depending on the cohesive characteristics of the social unit. Value can refer to:

1. A revenue source for the organization (Goyanes et al., 2020)

2. Access to people, stories, and communities that are newsworthy (Parks, 2020)

3. Controlling a particular market (Boyles, 2020)

4. Promoting democratic practices and culture (Anderson, 2018)

5. Advancing pro-social behaviors and ideals (Craig et al., 2020)

6. Maintaining a sense of local community (Poepsel, 2018)

7. Access to users that can craft compelling narratives that might gain an audience for the organization (Dunham, 2019) or

8. A combination of the above-listed definitions

These value arguments boil down to providing a reason to stay on the social network platform once setting up the account. This understanding of the value or benefit might come from using the site regularly. The concept of value also relates to people's perception of the data, information, and knowledge they find on a given social network.

These next three terms are the foundation of information studies. **Data** is the first of these terms that need to be addressed as it is individual quantitative or qualitative values associated with snapshots of reality during a given period. For example, the number 1600 has limited meaning to the average person. It is a single set of digits that lacks any additional data to suggest how to interpret the numbers. Data points fit nicely into a cell of a spreadsheet. Most of the time, the row and column header tell a person how to understand an individual data point.

Information is a string of data points that comes together to form a coherent idea. If data points are individual words, information is a sentence that is formed from those words. Much like regular sentences, actors are trained to read those strings as one coherent thought, based on past practice patterns. Going back to the 1600 example earlier, if the data points were put together to form 1600 Pennsylvania Ave., Washington, D.C. 20500, a person from the United States would generally recognize that string of data points as an address. Most of us were taught that the listed string of data points from this example was an address in elementary school. It's how we mail letters and get directions on our phones. Information alone does not help us navigate through the world.

This leads us to knowledge.

Knowledge is applying context to the presented information. The contextual understanding can come from a person's experience, education, training, or another form of socialization. People gain knowledge by being aware of the aspects of a situation that can be applied to their lives or familiarity with facts related to a topic or issue. Understanding the significance of the 1600 Pennsylvania Avenue example requires a background in U.S. Governance or watching mediated work about the President of the United States. That is the address for the White House.

Data, information, and knowledge are embedded in memetic communication. When a meme uses statistical figures to explain a particular position, it is using data points. Information only works in a meme if people know how to read it based on its formatting. The same can be said for knowledge within the meme, except that people need some experiences, training, or education to interpret what the knowledge means correctly.

Comprehending how these four listed factors (a critical mass of users; diversity of experience, opinions, and expressions; meaningful interactions through thoughtful engagements; underlying systematic value based in data, information, and knowledge) help transmit memes far and wide allows scholars in this field and therapeutic professionals to have better dialogues about how memetic artifacts can express the social-psychological states of social networks and its membership. This knowledge level also allows everyday Internet users to understand what the memetic artifacts mean to their community or collective and let them create more powerful and meaningful memes.

ERVING GOFFMAN & MEMETIC STRUCTURES

Erving Goffman's work in social interactions would seem to be useful in addressing the power of memetic communities. Goffman's (2008) first book, *The Presentation of Self in Everyday Life*, gives us a foothold of understanding these structures as an influential part of the socialization process that many people have when connecting with others online. He was a Canadian sociologist famous for his work on **symbolic interactionism**, which essentially looks at how social structures and the interactions within those social structures influence the advancement of the individual's perceptions of themselves, their personality, and their ability to define themselves within society. A reasonable interpretation of memetic communities depends on an analysis of Goffman's various theories in social psychology as they relate to both memetic communication and the social structures that support such communication.

Goffman's work was grounded in the human need to recognize others within society and maintain a sense of social order through civic rituals. Both of these concepts can be expressed in how we perform in front of others. These public, semi-private, and private actions form the foundation of what we understand as a society and all of the institutions that we consider supporting this concept of society (e.g., schools, churches, the media, and the government). Goffman framed these actions under his dramaturgical theory. It was in this theory that he argued William Shakespeare was right when Shakespeare wrote this classic monologue for Jaques in Act II, Scene VII of *As You Like It*,

> "All the world's a stage, And all the men and women merely players; They have their exits and their entrances, And one man in his time plays many parts..."

Social interactions define all aspects of society as past interactions form the foundations for the current state of society and man's future.

To properly place these rituals within the context of memetic structures, it is essential to apply one additional concept from dramaturgical theory, the idea of face-work. Goffman initially explained that **face-work** focused on how the non-verbal elements of interaction influenced a person's social identity construction. Face-work is commonly applied differently as it traditionally deals with face-to-face interactions as they impact interpersonal interactions and the structure of social norms within society. Face-work still works in memetic structure if we understand what is lost in a lack of face-to-face interaction, the complexity of memetic artifacts more than makes up for it. It is not a perfect substitution, but it gives a sense of nuance to the communication and interactions within the memetic structure if we understand that memes can also address members' social standings within the community or collective. Face-work helps explain that memetic communication is a performance that can change based on the meaning that the actors' place on others, the social network they are in, the time they are acting, and their view of society.

There are seven parts to the dramaturgical theory that connects well with the role that memes play in any social network. Actors within any social network believe in the part that they think they are playing within the social unit. This **belief** factors into how they present themselves. Memes can act as a shorthand for this presentation and for the techniques that they use to control the audience's perceptions of their performance (otherwise known as their **mask** or front-stage actions). Actors will also highlight critical aspects of their performance to transmit something to the audience. Goffman referred to this action as a dramatic realization. Actors also must present an **idealized representation** of their activities within society (think of the Instagram picture of the "perfect" Christmas, vacation, meal, or personal look) to strengthen their performance within the community or collective. Actors will recognize which social network they are in and attempt to maintain some form of **expressive control** to present the correct messaging to the social network. These actions are done to prevent transmitting an incorrect social message to the network (avoiding **misrepresentation**). Finally, the actor must conceal their true feelings, activities, and thoughts away from the community or collective (**mystifying** their private selves' by avoiding revealing these things in front of the rest of the social network).

Memes do much of the front-stage actions for actors. The messages' complexity within memes highlights the critical themes that align with the actor's performance within the memetic structure. For example, suppose an actor within a memetic structure wants to present themselves as someone who cares for others. In that case, the actor could use the "Serious Heart Hands" meme shown in Figure 7 of this book to deliver that caring message so that members will accept it within the social network. If the same actor wanted to present themselves as somebody more sarcastic in nature, the "Feel the Burn" meme from Figure 8 should provide the right amount of snarkiness for any occasion.

THE THERAPEUTIC CONSIDERATION

Memetic structures adapt well to therapists who are comfortable with social-psychological practices. Applying the memetic structural models discussed in the chapter opens up additional conversations between the therapist and client to be framed as developing a paradigm of how the client believes that they connect with the memetic structures they interact with regularly. One great focusing question to ask that relates to memetic structures would be, "Show me a meme that has meaning to you and one of your friends online. What is it about this meme that is meaningful to the both of you?" This question forces the client to consider their relationship with others online.

Reframing the conversation based on the social implications of memes within a community requires the client to think about the communal voice within their social network. Two techniques can help this process. The first one is to ask the client to, "Pick a person you consider to be wise online that you communicate with regularly. Please show me a meme that they frequently use. What does the person mean when they use it?" Answering this question can show the client how their interactions work within a social network. Another discussion point could be: "Pick a person that you consider popular online that you have had some interactions with. Tell me how they use memes online." Starting a conversation about this topic could help the client be more comfortable with day-to-day interactions with others, both online and face-to-face, by allowing them to critically consider their socialization methods.

Considering the collective model of memetic structures is more analytical. A straightforward way to answer this analysis is asking, "What would be considered a good meme to your friends online?" If the client is considering the question carefully, they might say, "It depends on which group of friends." This opening allows the therapist to discuss the different memetic structures they are connected to online. Follow-up questions can address how they define the other collectives that the client belongs to and which characteristics they believe connect most with their belief system and values.

Works Cited

Al-Taie, M. Z., & Kadry, S. (2017). Information diffusion in social networks. In *Python for Graph and Network Analysis* (pp. 165-184). Springer.

Anderson, C. W. (2018). Journalism as Procedure, Journalism as Values. *Journalism, 20(1), 8-12. doi:10.1177/1464884918806732*

Balsamo, D., Gelardi, V., Han, C., Rama, D., Samantray, A., Zucca, C., & Starnini, M. (2019). Inside the Echo Chamber: Disentangling network dynamics from polarization. *arXiv preprint arXiv:1906.09076.*

Barberá, P. (2018). Explaining the Spread of Misinformation on Social Media: Evidence from the 2016 U.S. Presidential election. Retrieved December 23, 2020, from: http://pablobarbera.com/static/barbera-CP-note.pdf

Barnes, J.A. (1972). *Social Networks.* Addison-Wesley Modular Publications. 1972(26)

Boulianne, S., Koc-Michalska, K., & Bimber, B. (2020). Right-wing Populism, Social Media and Echo Chambers in Western Democracies. *New Media & Society*, 22(4), 683-699.

Boyles, J. L. (2020). First-movers and Industry Shakeups: How public newspapers define value. *Newspaper Research Journal, 41*(2), 231-245. doi:10.1177/0739532920919824

Brass, D. J., & Borgatti, S. P. (2019). Multilevel Thoughts on Social Networks. In S. E. Humphrey & J. M. LeBreton (Eds.), *The Handbook of Multilevel Theory, Measurement, and Analysis* (p. 187–200). doi:10.1037/0000115-009

Craig, C. M., Brooks, M. E., & Bichard, S. (2020). Prosocial Consumer Socialization: How socialization agents impact prosocial attitudes and behavior. *Atlantic Journal of Communication*, 1-15.

Crossley, N., & Ibrahim, J. (2012). Critical Mass, Social Networks and Collective Action: Exploring student political worlds. *Sociology*, 46(4), 596-612.

Dosono, B., & Semaan, B. (2019, May). Moderation Practices as Emotional Labor in Sustaining Online Communities: The case of AAPI identity work on Reddit. In *Proceedings of the 2019 CHI Conference on Human Factors in Computing Systems* (pg. 1-13).

Dunham, R. S. (2019). Keys to Effective Journalism in the Multimedia Era. *Multimedia Reporting*, 23-39. doi:10.1007/978-981-13-6163-0_2

Geertz, C. (1973). *The Interpretation of Cultures* (Vol. 5019). Basic books.

Gibson, W. (1998). *Neuromancer.* Penguin Books.

Goffman, E. (2008). *The Presentation of Self in Everyday Life.* Anchor Books.

Goyanes, M., Rodriguez-Castro, M., & Campos-Freire, F. (2020). Value and Intelligence of Business Models in Journalism. In J. Vaizquez-Herrero, S. Direito-Rebollal, A. Silva-Rodriguez, & X. Lopez-Garcia (Eds.), *Journalistic Metamorphosis* (pp. 171-184). Springer Link.

Granovetter, M. (2005). The Impact of Social Structure on Economic Outcomes. *Journal of Economic Perspectives, 19*(1), 33-50.

Hill, L. B., & McGrath, J. M. (2008). Communication within the Triadic Context: Intercultural Prospects. *Intercultural Communication Studies, 17*(4), 53–67.

Jones, R. (2018). *Gif Wars.* Retrieved December 20, 2020, from: https://web.archive.org/web/20201220183735/https://ls2lnm.wordpress.com/2018/02/05/gif-wars/

Kowert, R. (Ed.). (2020). *Video Games and Well-being.* Springer International Publishing.

Liu, Y. H. (2020). From Critical Mass to Key Players: A Network Approach to Platform Design. *Available at SSRN 3492281.*

Maya-Jariego, I., Letina, S., & Tinoco, E. G. (2020). Personal Networks and Psychological Attributes: Exploring individual differences in personality and sense of community and their relationship to the structure of personal networks. *Network Science, 8*(2), 168-188.

McLean, P. (2016). *Culture in Networks*. John Wiley & Sons.

Min, S. J., & Wohn, D. Y. (2020). Underneath the Filter Bubble: The Role of Weak Ties and Network Cultural Diversity in Cross-Cutting Exposure to Disagreements on Social Media. *The Journal of Social Media in Society, 9*(1), 22-38.

Parks, P. (2019). The Ultimate News Value: Journalism textbooks, the U.S. Presidency, and the normalization of Donald Trump. *Journalism Studies, 21*(4), 512-529. doi:10.1080/1461670x.2019.1686413

Poepsel, M. (2019). Community and Small-Town Journalism. *The International Encyclopedia of Journalism Studies*, 1-7. doi:10.1002/9781118841570.iejs0120

Reese, S. D. (2010). Finding Frames in a Web of Culture: The case of the war on terror. In *Doing News Framing Analysis* (pg. 33-58). Routledge.

Ross, J. M. (2018). *The Role of Public Libraries in Rural Communication Infostructure* (Doctoral dissertation, University of Alabama Libraries).

Schroeder, J. (2020). Free-Expression Rationales, Truth, and the Marketplace of Ideas. *Available at SSRN 3606549.*

Shrivastava, G., Kumar, P., Ojha, R. P., Srivastava, P. K., Mohan, S., & Srivastava, G. (2020). Defensive Modeling of Fake News Through Online Social Networks. *IEEE Transactions on Computational Social Systems, 7*(5), 1159-1167.

Sicherl, P. (2019). Different Statistical Measures Create Different Perceptions of the Digital Divide. *The Information Society, 35*(3), 143-157.

Tilton, S. (2011). *Nanocelebrity: How to combine expertise with voice.* Retrieved December 26, 2020, from: https://www.researchgate.net/profile/Shane_Tilton/publication/297760728_Nanocelebrity_How_to_Combine_Expertise_with_Voice/links/56e31da908ae68afa10ca5e8/Nanocelebrity-How-to-Combine-Expertise-with-Voice.pdf

Tilton, S. (2020). *The Journalism Breakdown: Writing multimedia journalism content in an era of changing media systems & economic models.* CFSC Publishing.

Tönnies, F. (2017). *Community and Society.* Courier Corporation.

Westland, J. C. (2010). Critical Mass and Willingness to Pay for Social Networks. *Electronic Commerce Research and Applications, 9*(1), 6-19.

CHAPTER 4: MEMES & GESTALT THEORY

A wonderful thing happens when people come together and talk about memes in online social networks and face-to-face interactions. Discussions about these works parallel those conservations in front of those Magic Eye 3D Images at an art exhibit, mall, or vendor's booth somewhere in the world. People take some time, tilt their heads, look at the work from different angles, and speak about what they think they see. Unlike traditional works of art, the brain needs to pull together all parts of the image to see the subject hidden behind the digital noise and static.

Like those other digital works, memes can confuse the viewer and make them feel they have to fake an understanding of the works in order to fit in with the rest of the group. Viewers need to understand how to decode the meme, what the meme creator is trying to communicate via the meme, and understand what is contained in the layers of the meme to have a complete reading of a given meme. Pulling the various parts together within a meme to gain meaning from the work takes a different theoretical mindset and paradigm to see the digital world more clearly.

Once they have understood the power of interactions between memetic layers and memetic structures of communities and collectives, a scholar of memes should focus on how the parts of a meme speak to a given situation. At this point in the analysis, the discussion will turn to the classic visual communication theory, Gestalt Theory. We will go over what makes a memetic template and how that is different from a metameme. We will also discuss how Gestalt Theory helps explain the intertextual nature of memes. The chapter will conclude with the ways of seeing memetic content through the Law of Prägnanz and the groundbreaking work of John Berger.

DEFINING GESTALT THEORY

The easy way to begin a discussion about Gestalt Theory is to think about the patterns we notice throughout the day both online and in the real world. Pattern recognition is a powerful mental tool that allows one to explain the world with a clarity that would be lacking if it had not been discovered (Barkman, 2018). Patterns are defined by their common characteristics and how one should interpret the pattern's meaning. This connection between the characteristics of objects within the pattern and the pattern's meaning gets to Gestalt. **Gestalt Theory** simply stated that "the whole is more than the sum of its parts."

Imagine you are traveling in a car as a kid with your family. Looking out the window, you see a field of wheat, cows behind a wooden fence, tractors leaving a garage, and circular buildings with fans attached to them. It would be fair to look at all of the elements together and think you were looking at a farm. Seeing those elements trigger all of your thoughts and experiences associated with the farm, which is more than your thoughts and experiences with the fields, cows, fences, tractors, and silos put together. The composite of those elements crafts a mental narrative that allows you to make sense of that pattern.

It was a version of this experience that led the famous German psychologist Max Wertheimer to start to express the foundations of Gestalt Theory. After finishing a train trip in 1910, he bought a flipbook. This classic child's toy creates the illusion of motion by placing similar images back-to-back with minor differences between them. A person can animate a stick figure doing jumping jacks by drawing out the various visual forms that represent a state that the stick figure would be in when they are doing a jumping jack. Wertheimer would later argue that the eye takes in all of the visual information it is presented and attempts to make sense of how the various pieces of visual information connect (in the car example, the elements represent a farm, in the flipbook, the stick figure is doing jumping jacks) and make that the reality that the viewer experiences (Lester, 2013).

Moving away from these practical examples, those studying memes need to understand the Gestalt as their messages' complexity makes them an environment rich for pattern recognition. We began this analysis of memes' richness when going over the various layers that make them up. The textual, visual, compositional, and cultural layers are where most Gestalt patterns are found. How the people perceive the elements within those layers will help them decide what form the meme is taking. One of these forms is one that transcends the memetic form.

DEFINING METAMEMES

It is fair to argue that memes are iconic as they are easily recognizable artifacts of digital communication. Its form tends to be accessible to those who regularly use the Internet and interact with others. In fact, memes might be the most effective means of expression on social networks. They are a highly dense medium, as defined in the previous chapters. This density is due to the contextual, cultural, and social complexity of the messages within the medium. Internet interactions are often a simplified reduction of the real world. Memes tend to avoid becoming a diminished proxy of reality because of memetic communication's central tendencies to be self-referential and tied to other memetic content.

A select few memes explicitly reference memetic communication to the point that their existence is part of memetic culture's DNA. **Metamemes** are those memes that began as an implicit reference to how social network members should read them and then transcend beyond their original context. These memes are doing more than mimicking themselves. A good metameme tells something about memetic communication.

One of the examples of a metameme is the Impact typeface being connected with memetic content. Simply pasting the Impact typeface on top of an image has the viewer associate the work with other memes using the Impact typeface the person has seen in the past. Their experiences dictate how they should read the content they are viewing. The implicit reference comes from the pattern recognition of equating that font with other memes.

Moving to the cultural layer of a meme, Spongebob Squarepants has become a metameme due to increased use in other memetic artifacts. The tipping point that cemented his metameme status is when Nickelodeon turned the memes' original context into a series of toys. One can purchase Surprised Patrick, Handsome Squidward, and Spongebob (both in the Mocking form and the Imaaaaaaagination gesture). These toys reflect the trend of subcultures adapting the messages and content from popular culture sources to present those elements with a different message and purpose. Those elements become popular and crossover outside the subculture. They are repackaged by popular culture sources and sold to the masses (Chow, 2017).

Metamemes are useful to think about when discussing how memes reflect the Gestalt of the Internet. Memes present the viewer with a series of layers. Within those layers are the cultural and mediated patterns that inform the viewer how to interpret the presented information. Viewers are training to interpret those patterns via past socialization practices. Metamemes essentially act as a comment on those socialization practices and popular interpretations of other memetic artifacts. Understanding that metamemes exist allows the viewer to understand how memes work within communities throughout society.

METAMEMES VERSUS MEMETIC TEMPLATES

One of the common metamemes that Internet users will come across are memetic templates. **Memetic templates** are a basic construction that explains how the different layers are supposed to work together to create the meme. While memetic templates are a form of a metameme, these structural works tend not to help meme creators create new metamemes. There is no capability to incorporate novel critiques or analyses within the template, which is a core characteristic of a metameme. The differences between metamemes and templates are significant to note as both have essential functions in crafting memetic content.

We can focus on three meme generators as a way of explaining the difference between these two concepts. Users of ImgFlip, Kapwing, and MemeGenerator.net have access to an interface that essentially acts as a graphic design program that is limited to the typical aesthetic conditions found on most memes. These three sites have hundreds of the most common visual elements that appear in memetic content. People can add the text the best fits the situation they wish to comment on and download the final file.

Beyond the visual repository found on these sites, online meme template services show past examples of others' works using the same visual content. An archive of similar memes gives other users the syntax of applying the memes they create. Meme generators teach users the Internet's language by observing the most famous examples and giving users access to those specific works to apply for their purposes. As a point of comparison, metamemes direct people to memes' universal nature as they show general online usage. Creations from meme generators merely reflect on a snapshot of reality.

The application of the meme generator's formulations highlights the fundamental difference between these two concepts based on the power of memetic communication. Memetic templates are structurally significant in the development of memes, while metamemes are thematically significant. An example that clarifies the distinction further is the difference between the instructions one gets to put together a piece of Ikea furniture and the Ikea brand concept. Templates are those instructions. As described in the "Compositional Layer" section of the second chapter, they train people on putting the furniture together and generally how to use the furniture. Metamemes are in line with thinking about Ikea as a brand. People expect to build their furniture. There is an Ikea aesthetic that people enjoy, purchase, and add to their homes.

The simplicity of memetic templates has one final useful point to consider. Templates keep the meme's construction simple while allowing the meme creator to inject a complex message into the meme. The template acts as a metal skeleton that people can add the memetic layers on top of like a paper-mâché sculpture. Creativity is the driving force that makes the meme a novel form of communication and expression. Understanding metamemes allows a person to see behind the memetic layers' facade to understand how and why the meme creator put the meme together. This knowledge does not remove the appreciation of the meme creator's creativity and novel expression using the medium. Rather, the knowledge of metameme can help make the meme's message clearer to the audience. It helps demystify the presentation and removes the confusion of unclear elements within the meme. This clarification speaks to the next point that amplifies the parts of the meme to make the whole presentation memorial, powerful, and compelling.

DEFINING INTERTEXTUALITY

Intertextuality is a crucial component of understanding how the whole meme is an amplification of its parts. Graham Allen (2011) provides a good starting point to generally think about this concept. Allen rightly notes that the term is loaded down with some semantic weight to the point that it is hard to provide a clear denotative definition to the term. It is useful to think about **intertextuality** as the interplay between different cultural works within the memes that allows for a message to be decoded by the audience. The text in the intertextuality references the various books, magazines, graphic novels, movies, songs, plays, slogans, signs, and other popular culture works that a viewer would recognize and interpret a meaning from those works. Each of the different cultural works within the meme amplifies the message based on by adding context to the meme and the person viewing the work understanding the cultural significance of all of the cultural works that were added to the meme. In order to avoid William Irvin's (2004) main criticism of the term that intertextuality is mere "jargon that does not illuminate or elucidate but rather mystifies and obscures" and the term "should be stricken from the lexicon of sincere and intelligent humanists," we need to address three critical terms that are associated with both intertextuality and Gestalt Theory.

Using intertextuality in a discussion of Gestalt is vital because the interplay between various media sources allows meme creators to play with the audience's understanding of popular culture, specifically in memes that tend to jar the audience's view of those works.

Figure 9: An example of a troll quote. This memetic artifact depends on intertextuality and the audience's cultural capital to get the joke. The meme only trolls the viewer if they understanding that this meme is a mismatch of the Marvel Cinematic Universe, Star Wars, Hunger Games, Harry Potter, Lord of the Rings, The Chronicles of Narnia, Sherlock, Star Trek, and Doctor Who into one meme that misrepresents the significant of each of the elements reference within the meme. (Holly McCoy)

It would seem that text would be a reasonable place to start this discussion as the term is embedded in this concept. However, we need to sidestep text for two reasons. The first one is that text is one of those terms with a spectrum of meanings that can be commonly confused. It seems fair to avoid as much confusion as we can to clarify intertextuality as a concept. Secondly, text has a specific purpose and definition in the discussion of memes, as defined in the second chapter. Therefore, we need to use a secondary term for text. A good proxy for this term would be a linguistic sign, or just sign for short.

The popular method of defining a sign uses Ferdinand de Saussure's (2011) definition of the term, which combines two concepts: **signs** are crafted when a signified concept has a connection to some signifier in the form of a series of sounds, letters placed together to craft a word, or some other image that can act as a point of reference (e.g., think of an image of a fake heart representing love). An intertextual view of signs points to regularly seen cultural elements that have a deeper meaning to community members. Applying signs to Gestalt Theory forms the foundations of the patterns interpreted by viewers of the work. Placing different signs together can potentially change how the community interprets those signs.

A creator is the second concept we need to consider in order to define intertextuality. **Creators** are simply the actors responsible for using the tools of production to craft a mass-produced work that can be shared with others. We have talked about one type of creator in this book, the meme creator. Meme creators typically use the work of other creators to develop their memes. Often, a chain of creators influences future generations' works based on the techniques they used to produce media, the aesthetic decisions, the messaging, or other identifiable characteristics that others can duplicate in their work. An intertextual view of the creator would examine how that chain influenced their work. Examining the creator from a Gestalt perspective looks at how they put the parts together to amplify their message.

The last of the three relevant concepts is intent. The conceptual layer provides an excellent beginning to address this concept. The act of crafting a meme is deliberate, requiring time, effort, and attention to be accepted by the community successfully. Intent is the rationale of the meme creator to put the time, effort, and attention to craft their memes. Both Gestalt and the intertextuality would frame intent as aiding the creative spark in the meme's development.

The rationale for analyzing how signs, creators, and intent impact the Gestalt of a meme is that those three concepts drive the complexity of the messaging within a meme. Signs can have different meanings depending on the circumstances in which they are used. This potential confusion related to signs means that creators must attempt to clarify what the sign means when they are using them within a meme. Finally, the intent is the driving force that compels the creators to be transparent in their messaging. As presented in this section, intertextuality is simply part of the more considerable convergence that memes play in digital culture.

INTERTEXTUALLY VERSUS CONVERGENCE

A discussion about convergence seems to be the next logical point as convergence extends Gestalt Theory beyond what content creators are producing to the communication technologies content creators are using to produce their work. **Convergence** is the combination of media elements impacts the economy (in the form of cross-ownership of media companies), technology (in the form of new communication technology and convergent platforms), society (in the form of collaboration on projects), and culture (in the form of new multimedia content) in a manner beyond what one artist, organization, or tool could do alone (Jenkins et al., 2017). This concept works to expand the intertextuality discussion, as the term intertextuality traditionally represents content creators' ability to mash-up different text to craft a completely different message, intended for a different context than the original text was used in. Exploiting convergence can expand what intertextuality means, especially in how intertextuality relates to memetic communication.

Convergence addresses the impact of various creators working across different platforms (e.g., creating a meme on Imgur and the meme get shared on Facebook, Twitter, Instagram, and Reddit) and the messaging within the meme being reinterpreted by those various audiences, communities, and collectives. If a person becomes famous enough (either through their works or being an "Internet-famous personality" (Abidin, 2017) that would be recognized across platforms), convergence would represent working with others to craft new content for the Internet. Creative folks that are talented enough to present novel content that audiences enjoy might be asked to apply their talents to develop online media campaigns for companies.

Understanding convergence under Gestalt Theory is useful as the individual parts that come together to craft any piece of content (like a meme) will ensure that the final work is an amplification of those various parts that lead to the creation of that content (creators, technologies, platforms, and media elements). Convergence reinforces the idea that a meme is a carrier of complex communication constructions. Both intertextuality and convergence are new means of interpreting the power of the various forms of mediated communication. The influence of mass communication has been both overstated (e.g., the baseless criticisms that get levied against the "mainstream media" as opposed to the more rational criticisms connected with how money within the media presents crucial ethical dilemmas that are under-analyzed) and understated (e.g., how social media services represent a part of the global mass communication system) in popular discourses (Figenschou & Ihlebæk, 2019). Adding Gestalt Theory to this discussion helps rebalance the media's criticisms by the general public and allows for a more meaningful conversation about how people use media channels to express themselves.

THE FIGURE AND THE GROUND OF THE MEME

People are smart enough to understand how a meme is formed because they recognize the meme's figure's visual objects. Gestalt theory describes the **figure** as the composite of all interpretable, meaningful visuals within a visual work. Viewers of the meme can then separate the figure from elements with no significance to the meme's overall message. Those insignificant elements to the visual are known as the **ground**. Ground acts as a canvas that the meme exists on and allows that work to be seen.

The duality between the figure and the ground has been part of cognitive psychology for decades. There are four elements defined in this field of psychology that helps denote the difference. The **blurriness** within the image or message tends to point to the ground within the work. Blurriness (like seeing a blur in a photo) tells the viewer that the visual behind the blur is either unimportant or is merely supposed to be part of the background. Observing points of **contrast** within the visual will show the dividing lines between figure and ground. A person will tend to notice if one aspect of a meme is in front of an unusual shape or if it is in a bright color or if a piece of text is using a distinctive font. Those aspects of contrast allows the viewer to see the important parts of the meme, thus creating those dividing lines from the important (the figure) from the unimportant (the ground). **Size** and **separation** are the last two characteristics that will highlight the figure within the image. The larger elements within the work are understood by the viewer to be essential to the messaging within the meme, otherwise there would be no reason for those elements to be larger. Elements that are isolated from the rest of the graphic can also be viewed as essential if the viewer understands why those elements are separate from the rest of the parts of the meme (Grossberg, 2016).

Knowing the difference between the figure and the ground of the meme allows a person to filter out unnecessary information within the content. Much of this unnecessary information comes from the structural points of the meme discussed earlier in this book. These elements support the more meaningful visual communication that occurs within a meme. Eliminating the ground from the meme essentially erases what we would consider to make an image a meme. The nature of Internet interactions depends on this structure to make sense of the visual. They act as the aesthetic components that allow the viewer to read the meme with a similar mindset to the meme creator when they composed the meme.

Figure and ground are just two of the concepts embedded in Gestalt Theory that can help professionals decode the underlying messages within memes. Most of the other core theoretical components address how visual communication works are meaningful to an audience and allow for effective engagement between community members.

THE LAW OF PRÄGNANZ AND THE PERCEPTUAL GROUPINGS OF MEMES

One of the significant reasons that Gestalt Theory works well to deconstruct memes for therapeutic sessions is due to a central law within Gestalt. Specifically, the law of Prägnanz is a meaningful rule that helps put together the various discussion points from this chapter into a complete theoretical package. **Prägnanz** is a German word that basically means "good figure." The qualification that Gestalt theorists would point to in order to declare that a visual work has a good figure is its simplicity. This is because the brain prefers not to work so hard to translate visual information into meaningful knowledge. Several principles within the psychology of perception help us define a graphic as having a good figure (Cherry, 2019).

The best known of these characteristics is the law of proximity, which states that figures that are close together and share similar traits will appear to belong together. This law is one of the significant reasons that camouflage works in the wild. Creating a garment with shades of green and brown that match what one would see in a forest makes it easier for a person wearing that clothing to blend into the trees, bushes, and brush that are naturally found in that environment. Groups in a meme's figure give those objects similar properties in the viewer's mind. Another example of the role that proximity plays in affecting the reading of a piece of content is the "Don't Dead Open Inside" category of meme. The original context of this meme came from the "Walking Dead" TV series. The first episode showed a pair of doors with "Don't Dead" spray painted on the top of the doors and "Open Inside" on the bottom of the doors. It was supposed to be read "Don't Open, Dead Inside" but could be easily misread. This scene led to the memetic template based around that concept. A judgment can be made about what the meme creator thinks of particular ideas based on how they place them within a meme (Izakson et al., 2020).

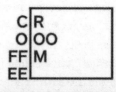

Figure 10: Two examples of the "Don't Dead Open Inside" memetic format. This memetic format depends on proximity to manipulate the central textual layer within a meme and show conflicting messaging based on badly placed words in a given visual space.

The law of **similarity** addresses that objects in the figure viewed as having collective, shared characteristics will be perceived as related. Similarity allows for baseline rhetorical arguments to be made within a meme through the meme creator, pointing out common connections between two subjects or highlighting differences. Any meme that compares and contrasts two or more subjects tends to use the law of similarity as the means of selecting those subjects. There are enough characteristics that those subjects share that the viewer will see a connection between those subjects.

Another Gestalt law that helps meme creators craft meaningful messages within their memes is the law of closure. **Closure** is the brain filling in missing pieces for an object in the figure. This additional information happens as we expect an object to be completed. This particular law forces the brain to make up for the gaps within the visual. **Continuity** works similarly: we are trained to see points in a figure that could be connected by a straight or curving line.

The last two of the Gestalt laws worth discussing in this chapter are based on the viewer's knowledge of how the world works. **Common fate** addresses the idea that objects that are together in a figure oriented the same way will move in the same direction. It is this law that creates the illusion of movement within the figure. **Past experience** focuses on that humans have been exposed to stimuli regularly and that stimuli influence our expectations of how we view the world. It is this law that allows a meme creator to change the way objects are perceived within a meme. Suppose Bert from our earlier example appears with Adolf Hilter, Osama bin Laden, Lee Harvey Oswald, and the Ku Klux Klan members. In that case, we will associate Bert with being evil. Flipping that script, posting Bert with Bob Ross, Mr. Rogers, Steve Irwin, Alex Trebek, and Tom Hanks would make Bert appear to be more wholesome. This technique related to the law of past experience is also called the **Halo Effect** (Pohl, 2016).

Factoring in these various Gestalt laws helps address a potential criticism of this book. We mentioned categorizing memes in the first chapter. We described the difficulty in crafting a memetic lexicon that would remain relevant after the book is published. Sites like Know Your Meme have the advantage of dynamically changing the website's organization based on new traits that memes might take on, but a book is a static object. Gestalt laws give the reader some enduring tools for how to group memes for memetic analysis and therapeutic sessions. As long as the person can argue how memes can be grouped and the characteristics that place those memes in a discreet group, they can begin to have intelligent conversations about what those memes mean.

JOHN BERGER AND THE WAYS OF SEEING MEMETIC CONTENT

John Berger was known for challenging the traditional assumption that scholars make about the art world by addressing how the audience views those works. His most famous work on visual communication (1972) is relevant to this discussion of memes for a simple reason. Berger's work is related to his passion of expanding the viewer and reader's understanding of the power of the visual medium. Seeking meaning in visual content is not an arena solely of art historians and visual scholars. Rather, having the critical tools to understand art and visuals should be available to us all. *Ways of Seeing* was a BBC series and best-selling book that focuses on how mass communication changed the public's view of artworks, the places that store and display these works, and the people who discuss them. John Berger was mainly critiquing European art in this groundbreaking work. However, scholars have applied his viewpoints to various other works of popular art and design.

A critical point in Berger's analysis of European art is that artists were focusing their creations around the concept of the viewer's perspective. He argues that this concept is unique to this genre of art. Artists in this genre considered the viewer as the beholder of a version of existence directed by the artist and experienced by the viewer of the work. This momentary snapshot of a shared reality allowed the artist to express, in Berger's words, "something meaningful" through whatever medium they worked with. The meaningfulness that Berger is referring to is the ability of the viewer of the work to find at least one element from the work that they can connect with as part of their daily existence. *Ways of Seeing* attempted to take classical paintings and other artworks from their metaphorically dusty shelves and give them life in the modern era of the 1970s.

Berger's scholarship is fitting to add to this chapter as he addresses a central truth in Gestalt Theory. The meanings explained by Gestalt Theory must fit the reality and the perspective of all people involved with the memetic artifact. Memes reproduce the experiences of a meme creator by allowing others to interpret that meaning of each of the meme's elements through a psychological reconstruction consistent with the practices described by Gestalt Theory.

A crucial argument that he makes in the book and the BBC series about the value of this knowledge is that by understanding how creative works are produced and reproduced, the work becomes more accessible to the audience. **Accessibility** has a multifaceted definition, including these implications:

1. a person can access seeing a meme through a variety of communication tools (e.g., computer, phone, tablet, and other smart devices),

2. the cultural significance or meaningfulness of any object within the meme can be made accessible through research tools (e.g., a search engine), and

3. the person can access their friends' and acquaintances' opinions and thoughts about the meme via online communication services (e.g., social media network).

Berger argues that these works (e.g., memes) have become demystified as they are "available in any size, anywhere, for any purpose." Any artistic works truly no longer exist in just one place and time. Artworks are not ephemeral or cut off from others due to where they are located. The Internet provides the structure to support an archive of the world's cultural bounty and others' means to see these creative works.

The last critical point that Berger makes about cultural works in the modern age is that the viewer sees such works within the context of their own lives. For example, if a person sees a meme on their phone, they can hand their phone to others to share that work face-to-face with somebody else. Or, viewing memes on a traditional computer screen means that they see those memes in the comfort of their own home or office. Berger emphasizes that point by stating that art was "only possible to see in the room where it was actually hanging. Now its image or detail of it, or the image of any other painting which is reproduced, can be seen in a million different places at the same time." There is no longer a uniqueness to the experience of viewing a creative work. It is accessible to a community or a collective for any purpose that a memetic structure wishes to use it for.

THE THERAPEUTIC CONSIDERATION

Applying Gestalt Theory to the therapeutic setting means that the therapist and the client are aware of the patterns within the memes and what those patterns mean regarding the expression of ideas, beliefs, values, and attitudes to a community. This chapter is merely a primer for Gestalt Theory. It would be beneficial for those interested in a deeper understanding of Gestalt to review Berger's work, along with psychologist Max Wertheimer's (2012) *On Perceived Motion and Figural Organization*, David W. Hamlyn's (2017) *The Psychology of Perception: A Philosophical Examination of Gestalt Theory and Derivative Theories of Perception*, Paul Martin Lester's (2020) *Visual Communication*, and Kurt Koffka's (2014) *Principles of Gestalt Psychology*.

Discussing the meaningful patterns within a meme requires excellent focus questions to help facilitate discussion between client and therapist. Five such are a helpful starting place, with the goal of understanding the client's view of those patterns. A higher-level question can be: "how would you describe the patterns within the meme?" This question's benefit is that it can frame the discussion toward the awareness of the pattern within the meme and then apply Gestalt Theory towards the meaningfulness of those patterns.

One way to connect Gestalt Theory with the psychological state of the client is to ask, "why does the template work for what you are trying to say?" Templates act as a part of the whole that is the meme. They balance between being the ground (the structure the rest of the meme is built on) and the figure (contextually important information). The previous question can be followed up with, "what content would you add to this meme to better express yourself?" Both questions address how the structure of the meme helps facilitate online interactions.

Meme creators can be asked, "what inspired the placement of the objects within the meme?" Questions of this nature allow the client to explain the artistic process and flesh out the creativite areas that they might not have addressed verbally before or even codified in a meaningful way. Adding Gestalt law in the analysis and discussion point will allow a more thoughtful conversation when focusing on the meme.

Another analytical question based on Gestalt Theory that can kickstart a great session is, "how does the meme demystify the message it is trying to transmit?' The purpose of asking this question is to approach clear communication practices online. Bullet points addressing this dialogue are often found in the Gestalt laws mentioned earlier in this chapter.

Finally, a solid focusing question related to this topic is "what visuals define the memes that you use regularly?" This question is meant to go beyond the cultural components found in most memes.

Also, this conversation point is not meant to talk about the meme from the vantage point of an art critic. Pattern recognition is part of Gestalt Theory. Questions of this nature help the therapist interject what they know about Gestalt Theory into the session in a way that does not overwhelm the client with information nor make the client feel ignorant. These types of accessible questions should allow for an open dialogue between the two parties.

Works Cited

Abidin, C. (2017, January 20). *Micro-microcelebrity: Famous babies and business on the internet*. LSE Research Online. http://eprints.lse.ac.uk/76135/.

Allen, G. (2011). *Intertextuality*. Routledge.

Barkman, R. (2018, January 18). *See the World Through Patterns*. Psychology Today. https://www.psychologytoday.com/us/blog/singular-perspective/201801/see-the-world-through-patterns.

Cherry, K. (2019, November 5). *Gestalt Laws of Perceptual Organization and Our Perception of the World*. Verywell Mind. https://www.verywellmind.com/gestalt-laws-of-perceptual-organization-2795835.

Chow, Y. F. (2017). Subcultures: Role of media. *The International Encyclopedia of Media Effects*, 1-11.

de Saussure, F. (2011). *Course in General Linguistics*. Columbia University Press.

Figenschou, T. U., & Ihlebæk, K. A. (2019). Media Criticism from the Far-right: Attacking from many angles. *Journalism Practice, 13*(8), 901-905.

Grossberg, S. (2016). Cortical Dynamics of Figure-ground Separation in Response to 2D Pictures and 3D Scenes: How V2 combines border ownership, stereoscopic cues, and Gestalt grouping rules. *Frontiers in Psychology, 6*, 2054.

Hamlyn, D. W. (2019). T*he Psychology of Perception: A philosophical examination of gestalt theory and derivative theories of perception*. Routledge.

Irwin, W. (2004). *Against Intertextuality. Philosophy and Literature 28*(2), 227-242. doi:10.1353/phl.2004.0030.

Izakson, L., Zeevi, Y., & Dino, L. (2020). Attraction to Similar Options: The Gestalt law of proximity is related to the attraction effect. *PsyArXiv*. doi:10.31234/osf.io/jvcg5

Jenkins, H., Ito, M, & boyd, d. (2017). *Participatory Culture in a Networked Era: A conversation on youth, learning, commerce, and politics*. Polity Press.

Koffka, K. (2014). *Principles of Gestalt Psychology*. Mimesis Edizioni.

Lester, P. M. (2020). *Visual Communication: Images with messages*. Nelson Education.

Pohl, R. F. (2016). *Cognitive Illusions: Intriguing phenomena in judgement, thinking and memory*. Psychology Press.

Wertheimer, M. (2012). *On Perceived Motion and Figural Organization*. MIT Press.

CHAPTER 5: MEMETIC CREATIVE CONTENT

The previous four chapters of this book have essentially looked at memes as Internet black boxes of communication. They are the means people use to express themselves on social media, elsewhere online, and in the real world. Memes are adapted based on situation, community, and context. Online community members adjust the memes as needed to present a clear message to the rest of the community. Throughout the discussion about community members, meme creators have been addressed as roughly the same as posters. Posters simply use the memetic content that meme creators make.

This book is not the best venue to discuss the nature of creativity. There are better experts in this field that can speak to the psychological, sociological, cultural, artistic, and performative nature of human creativity. Rather, this chapter is influenced by Patricia Townsend's (2019) *Creative States of Mind*, John Cleese's (2020) *Creativity: A Short & Cheerful Guide*, Doron Meir's (2018) *Workflow: A Practical Guide to the Creative Process*, House Industries' (2017) *The Process is the Inspiration*, and (my personal favorite) Austin Kleon's (2012) *Steal Like an Artist*. These authors' works can address the creative mind's innerworkings far better than a general primer of memes could hope to.

We will look at the three cornerstones in the meme-creation process and conclude by addressing the theoretical connection between visual communication and the development of creative content with Edward Tufte's work. This analysis will be followed by how to use the knowledge of the creative content creation process in a therapeutic session.

DEFINING CREATIVE CONTENT

Memes are more than files that are shared among people online. These digital works start as the ones and zeros of binary code in a computer representing a snapshot of reality in the analog world. Scholars who study memetic communication tend to address more than just the messaging within the meme or even how people use it. It is essential to highlight this creative aspect of memes when addressing the psychology of memetic communication. This content provides insight into the mind of the creator.

The concept of **creative content** has a few characteristics that distinguish it from the wide variety of files one can find online. Creative content is an exhibition of connections between two or more works of popular culture, people recognized by community members, topics that the community is familiar with, issues that are open to community debate, events that community members are participating in, or points-of-interest that speak to the spirit of the community (Askin & Mauskapf, 2017; Sugihartati, 2020). These connections help community members gain new insights into what is happening in their communities and the rest of society. Connections of this nature can be expressed visually (e.g., showing a person performing a risky action and following the show of that action with a video of pallbearers dancing beside a coffin), textually (e.g., the set-up to most stand-up comedy is built on this idea), aurally (e.g., explaining that most pop songs are built on a four-chord progression and performing a melody of those songs to prove that point), and interactively. Creative content allows the artist to apply various techniques to express their vantagepoint of the world better.

Another characteristic that defines creative content is that these works add to the cultural legacy of a given community (Gehman & Soublière, 2017). Artists use techniques and tools to express themselves and add their voices to the social network's artistic dialogue. These creations potentially become additional platforms for community members to express themselves without modifying or remixing the original work for new social situations and interactions.

A final characteristic that can help denote creative content is that it tends to be the output of the creative process crafted by a skilled worker in a given field (Toubia, 2018). This notion of the output of the creative process is a useful one for discussion about memes. The outcome is typically the summary of the artist's viewpoint of a given subject, during a given period of time, based around a variety of cultural and social influences. A better under-standing of what the summary means can be found in reference materials not directly connected with the meme (e.g., Know Your Meme website). The short explainer provides key references that create a connotative definition for the meme. This output is also a novel portrayal of reality that the artist synthesizes and presents on a given medium to benefit an audience. Both the novelty of the production and how the creation summarizes the artist's views can be studied in memetic communication.

These characteristics of creative content reflect the produc-tion process most content creators used when developing their work. Most content producers divide the process into three modes. There's the pre-production process in which all of the planning for the content is done. This section is followed by the actual produc-tion work in the form of recording, performing, or any other action that can be captured with media tools like phones, cameras, dig-ital audio recorders, or similar devices. Finally, a content creator will edit the various media pieces to form creative content in the post-production phase. The rest of this chapter will address these three phases (pre-production, production, and post-production) of the creative content creation process.

PRE-PRODUCTION: TO INSPIRE

The pre-production process for most meme creators really exists in the inspiration phase of creativity. Inspiration is looking over the past cultural works, the techniques for crafting content, and the technologies that enable creating new content that speaks to the artist's viewpoint. A meme creator decides which of those elements allows them to present their view of the world based on what is happening within their community and the culture and society at large. Laura Jordan Bambach, Mark Earls, and Scott Morrison (2018) address the four aspects that bring inspiration to content creators.

The most significant point of inspiration that artists have is when they can divide broad social and cultural issues into more manageable pieces that are easy to address. They refer to this ability as **hacking**. Meme creators view the world's challenges and use mediated works to break them down into memes that can get to the heart of those matters. Memes can be a short-term solution to a problem by making the community aware of an issue they need to resolve (e.g., posting a meme that highlights hunger within a local community) or a long-term tactic to work on broader community concerns (e.g., the "Ice Bucket Challenge"). Hacking is a continuous process as the community will always experience issues that its members need to address.

Meme creators also tend to have a vision of the world that requires their community and its members to learn what is happening in society, unlearn habits and behaviors that are harmful and ineffective for working with others, and relearning how the institutions and organizations function in the modern world. The term that gets applied to this aspect of inspiration is referred to as **teaching**. It explores the world as a learning environment where all lessons are either informal (e.g., a casual conversation about voting during an election) and formal (e.g., a structured argument supporting changes to voting in your state).

The third aspect of inspiration is that most artists have a notebook or folders filled with half-formed ideas or sentences that act as the origin point for much of their creative work. So the artist does not need to start from scratch when creating something new. This useful guide is how artists make something when they might not have a spark of immediate inspiration to work from.

The last aspect of inspiration is the one that directly relates to memetic communication; as it addresses how artists "elegantly steal" from others' creative works. This aspect is not the same as plagiarism or even copyright infringement. Bambach, Earls, and Morrison refer to this aspect as being a **thief**, but they are using the term in the same manner as Austin Kleon in his book *Steal Like an Artist*. It is understanding how the best artists in their field craft their works and using the same techniques. This aspect is not new. The most renowned artists from the Renaissance (Leonardo da Vinci and Michaelangelo Buonarotti, to name a couple) began their careers creating forgeries of famous works during that historical period (Keats, 2013). The reason that forgeries are being used in this case (instead of copies) is that who we consider the masters of their craft sold fake antiques. For example, Michelangelo crafted a sculpture entitled "Sleeping Cupid" that he buried in the ground for a couple of months in order to convince the collector of the time that it was a genuine Roman artifact. It was discovered to be a fraud by a cardinal, who wanted to meet the artist (Coates, 2016). It was through this process that they developed their skills to become the artists the world knows today. These four aspects of inspiration are vital in this discussion of the crafting of memetic creative content. It helps explain how meme creators can do more with the medium than merely express their beliefs and values to the community.

CODING PERSONAL EXPERIENCES

A meme creator's ability to craft a meme based on their personal experiences is still grounded in the collective's formatting of memetic artifacts. There are aspects of culture that form this foundation and help maintain social norms within these digital expressions (Nissenbaum & Shifman, 2018). A successful and effective meme is only spread throughout a memetic structure if it speaks to the rest of the community or collective. Therefore, the individual's experiences presented in the meme must have a level of generality to resonate with others.

This meme's ability to resonate with the memetic structure forces the meme creator to consider several factors before sharing a memetic artifact. When posting a meme for a collective, the meme creator must think about the common characteristics that bind the collective together. Hitting on those wavelengths makes it more likely that the meme will spread. Success of memes within a community depends on speaking to the human condition in a novel manner. Like stand-up comedians make an audience laugh, meme creators focus on either the nuances of everyday life or behaviors that make us human.

Before any of the meme's actual production happens, a meme creator must decide what messages fit with the meme's context and which template best serves the message they are trying to communicate. Most memetic templates are pre-loaded with meaning based on how they have been used in the past. Meme creators must recognize what meaning the template holds to communicate their message effectively. For example, the Galaxy Brain template is a recognized means among meme creators of highlighting the logical superiority of various connected elements or concepts. If a meme creator wanted to highlight the logical progression of different meme templates, the Galaxy Brain template would seem to be a reasonable one to use.

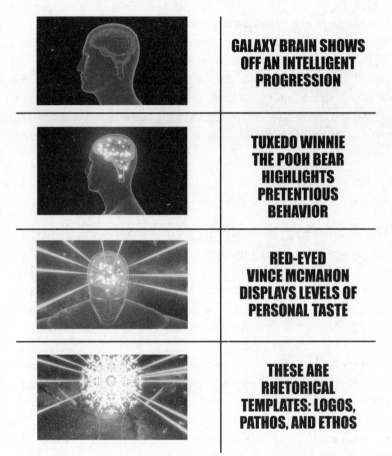

	GALAXY BRAIN SHOWS OFF AN INTELLIGENT PROGRESSION
	TUXEDO WINNIE THE POOH BEAR HIGHLIGHTS PRETENTIOUS BEHAVIOR
	RED-EYED VINCE MCMAHON DISPLAYS LEVELS OF PERSONAL TASTE
	THESE ARE RHETORICAL TEMPLATES: LOGOS, PATHOS, AND ETHOS

Figure 11: A Galaxy Brain memetic resource denoting the contextual differences between a few memetic templates. Sources: lsmft (CC-0), https://blendswap.com/blend/8395, mahesh (CC-BY), https://blendswap.com/blend/13180, egil sjøholt (CC-0) https://pexels.com/photo/silhouette-photography-of-person-under-starry-sky-1906658/, Felix Mittermeier (CC-0) https://pexels.com/photo/starry-night-sky-1205301/ Free Nature Stock (CC-0) https://pexels.com/photo/photography-of-stars-and-galaxy-1376766, ESA/Hubble (CC-BY) https://esahubble.org/images/heic0706a/ and @desplesda (https://twitter.com/desplesda/status/1360743216832606210)

Lastly, consider that a meme creator might not care if the rest of the community, collective, or society views the topic or issues described in the meme the same way they do. This level of freedom is useful to think about from the vantage point of a scholar of memes as it points to the intent behind creating the meme. It can be a personal expression with no filter. Therapeutic professionals can use this artifact to start a conversation about beliefs, values, and behaviors.

PRODUCTION: TO CREATE

Meme creators have some advantages over other content creators. The barriers between the inspiration for their creation and its creation in some form, either in the real world or online, are few. This lack of creative friction is due in part to the easy use of production tools needed to craft such works. This chapter will address these tools a little later. The focus now is how one creates a meme that resonates with one's audience.

Memes are incredibly effective at connecting with an audience if they are a novel expression about a timely issue affecting a community, highlight an essential fact about a topic of current communal discussion, or strike at the membership's prevailing emotional state. Any one of these three outcomes requires the meme creator to be aware of the community's current condition and news of the world. In this way, the creative process relates to being attuned to cultural and social events to the point that their perceptions allow them to address these touchstones creatively and thoughtfully. Therefore, producing memes requires the meme creator to connect those events to the community or collective to hit one of the three outcomes in an inventive way.

This level of connection also requires the meme creator to know what signs speak to community members. A shared social experience could change that sign's meaning within the community, or the collective might have a different reading of popular culture works. Meme creators need to be keen on how members will read the signs within the meme.

Creating finally requires the meme creator to focus their message into something that can be expressed within a meme, the time to produce a meme of appropriate quality (e.g., shitposting is built on quickly creating low-quality content to connect to a memetic structure on a deeper level (Holm, 2017)), and the energy to see to the completion of the meme. These three attributes (focus, time, and energy) are also the foundations to complete any project (Meredith, Shafer, & Mantel Jr, 2017). This comparison is not to say that memes are merely the grunt work in maintaining a social network's cohesive nature. Rather, memes should be seen as a communication task that helps everybody within the memetic structure feel like they are part of a collective whole.

Understanding that the tools of production allow meme creators to place their focus, time, and energy to address community members about timely topics and issues in a language that they recognize means that the meme creator can be more effective using those tools to express themselves and get their message across to the community or collective. How meme creators use these tools is worth our time to discuss.

TOOLS OF PRODUCTION

One of the defining characteristics of the production tools that meme creators use is that all these tools typically exist in a computer. Images that are used in the memes most of the time come from other creators. Therefore, they are already a digital file or can be easily captured by recording content from other sources.

The font faces are also easily shared files. Finally, software compresses the various layers together into one complete meme that can be shared.

This self-contained production suite means that meme creators can quickly create content representing the "up-to-the-minute" community reactions to public events. A simple example of this quick response by online communities is the Bernie Sanders memes. The most popular of these memes were circulated following the Biden inauguration. The general public saw the Senator from Vermont at the event wearing the same brown overcoat that he usually would put on for an outdoor winter event and a pair of hand-knitted mittens, sitting alone holding a manila envelope. Sanders was immediately placed into hundreds of famous scenes from movies and television shows. These memes were followed by a wave of memes depicting him in more familiar settings.

Figure 12: A series of #SitWithBernie memes after the Biden Inauguration produced by Ohio Northern University.

One of the significant factors contributing to these cultural works' rapid production is that meme creators do not need a wide variety of skills to craft a meme that reflects the message they want to express. Most of the meme generators discussed earlier allow for the simple combination of visual content with a textual layer on top. The #SitWithBernie memes require superimposing Bernie Sanders with a transparent background on top of another image. The template is nothing more than a singular graphic. The meme's cultural layer does most of the heavy lifting, turning this work into a meaningful image to the audience. The meaningfulness of #SitWithBernie goes beyond what is commonly referred to as "a mood." The meme resonated with people as Sanders was being iconically comfortable during a historical event. The lack of fashionableness in Sanders' was made wholesome due to the backstory of Bernie's mittens. They were given to him by Jen Ellis, a second-grade teacher would knits gloves as a fundraiser for LGBTQ youth group. Therefore, the cultural layer (in addition to the visual representation of Sanders in the meme) makes the meme meaningful and easily shared on social media.

For more complex memes, meme creators might use some graphic design programs to craft the final digital work. Adobe Creative Cloud Suite tends to be an advanced version of the websites and free software that meme creators begin their memetic careers with or even still use if they are comfortable with what the software produces. An invisible part of this process is how the software influences the meme creator's ability to create memes. Developers choose how the users interact with the software. This mental construction of the world means that developers must have a paradigm of expected user behaviors. Adobe software tends to use traditional metaphors in the user interfaces. Photoshop (Adobe's photo editing software) places the user on top of a virtual light table when crafting images. The cropping tool's icon, for example, is a proxy for the cropping tool that editors would use in a news-room or print media organization. The way users interact with this digital tool is similar to how their analog predecessors would use a marking frame or adjustable easel to mark up photographs.

Considering the production tools that meme creators use to craft memes gets to the heart of the creative process. While there are limited barriers to creating a meme, the process itself has social and cultural complications that can impact their ability to communicate effectively with others. Scholars of memetic culture should recognize that memes are a collaboration between the meme creator, their production tools, and the memetic structure that the meme creator connects with to share their memes.

POST-PRODUCTION: TO SHARE

The final step in the creation of memes is the post-production. Post-production for memetic content happens when the meme creator shares their work with their communities and collectives. Naturally, the post-production of a mediated project depends on the editing and distribution of the content. However, memetic content is produced in the editing and layering of media within the image file, video, or something else that acts as the meme creator's canvas.

The nature of social networks means that all forms of content are expected to be shared with friends and followers connected to the meme creator. There are two aspects worth noting about the process of sharing memes as it relates to memetic content. The first is the sense of place that memes exist in when they are shared via social networks. Unless they come from an external site, that digital content exists nowhere except on a server acces-sible through the right permissions and metadata references. Even memes stored outside a given social media service depend on social media platforms not to block the content. This acknowledgment means that meme creators should recognize the limited agency they have compared to the businesses that run these services.

The second critical point about sharing memes via social networks is that those memes are framed within the social network structure. Often, the first exposure for memes shared on social networks comes from the nodes on those networks. Groups, pages, and hashtags act as the spreading points for memes. The meme's connection to nodes online means that those memes are associated with all of the positives and negatives related to those nodes. For example, Pepe the Frog has a negative reputation because of its association with white supremacist and alt-right groups.

Sharing only works if there is a memetic structure that supports the work's transmission via its network. The two types of memetic structures will tend to share memes differently. As communities thrive on social interactions and the bond created by those actions, meme creators typically depend on their content to be meaningful so that community members are more likely to share their work. Memes that successfully spread in these social systems speak to their members' humanity and community members' values.

Placement within the category makes the meme more likely to be shared throughout the memetic structure. Understanding what attributes of the classification of memes will enable the meme creator to express their position clearly while hitting the points that bind the collective means that the meme creator must be careful in crafting the work to address both of those issues. Unlike posting a meme in a community, the collective can filter content that doesn't meet their ideals . Posting a meme about dogs traditionally would not work in a group that focuses on cat-related content, for example. Any memes about dogs on a cat-centric online group is more likely to be ignored, downvoted, or removed if the group does not allow non-cat content.

SOCIAL MEDIA

We should conclude this section on the creative process by addressing the central system for inspiring, creating, and sharing memes across the Internet. Social media services are the nexus of memetic culture online. Facebook, Twitter, Reddit, Instagram, and the other wide variety of platforms users flock to embrace the digital format in its native environment daily. It is online that memes go through the "Four Phases of Memetic Works" described by Shifman (2014) and discussed in this book's first chapter.

The meme's original context can be shared by a community member to the rest of the community or added to a collective's collection of memes in a given category. The community or collective then can mimic or remix the meme to craft a newer version. The more unique versions of the meme there are, the better the meme's chances of being selected by the community or collective to represent a discrete idea. Finally, the meme can escape the community or collective and be recognized by the general public as it reaches the hypermemetic stage of memetic content.

Social media adds to the complexity of memetic artifacts. Those services add additional information to the memes' contextual and cultural layers and can impact the memes' performative and rhetorical layers. By members adding different visual assets to a version of the meme, the community or collective injects or substitutes the cultural capital needed to decode the messaging within the meme. Those adjustments will also impact how community members will use this meme and the meme's context as part of the memetic structure's interactions. How a meme is performed within the collective or community can be enhanced by additional textual and visual assets.

The dynamic part of this entire process is that members can add comments, reactions, and other social media content to adjust how the community or collection defines the meme. Community members can hijack a meme to interject with some other message. This type of hijacking is similar to what happens to hashtags on sites like Twitter. Corporations can adopt public hashtags to promote their brands. In contrast, the general public can hijack corporate hashtags for social causes or to troll companies.

As discussed in this book's preface, memes are one of the natural end-results of Internet communication. Social media makes memes more accessible to the general public, thereby increasing the spread across a wide variety of communities and collectives. Each of those memetic structures determines how members read and use these digital works.

EDWARD TUFTE AND THE BEAUTIFUL EVIDENCE OF MEMES

Discussing memes as part of a more significant content production process would need a strong theorist who can get to the heart of what makes a meme an effective messaging tool. One scholar who works at the intersection of design, information, communication, and engagement is Edward Tufte. Tufte is best known for the phrase "death by PowerPoint" to describe information overload within a visual medium. His scholarship is useful in examining the creative process of those talented people that develop memes.

One of his best-known books is *Beautiful Evidence* (2006), which deals with how people practice useful design techniques to clearly express their messages. He explores the theories that drive these works of visual communication. Tufte has argued that "evidence is evidence" regardless of the format in which it is presented. This suggests that meme creators presenting an argument that is designed to persuade an audience need to clarify the evidence for their case, as well as the knowledge necessary to grasp the key points of the argument. The meme creator can use the meme's visual composition to fulfill these criteria.

The heart of Tufte's writing puts a premium on simplifying the message for clarity. It is this principle that speaks to the paradox of effective memetic content. A dynamic meme that finds success outside the community or collective that started it must be simple enough to be understood by various people while being complex enough to be meaningful to the people who see it. This middle ground is hard to reach, so when a meme hits both of those criteria, it tends to go viral (Castaño Diaz, 2013; Bebić & Volarevic, 2018; Coscia, 2014).

Memetic content creation processes tend to be as diverse as the meme creators that craft them. Tufte's principles still hold as the more popular memes within a given community or collective will have the paradox present in their design. In his newest book (2020), *Seeing with Fresh Eyes*, there is an argument that viewers need to question the relationship between the space used to craft memes and what meaning is gained by people using those spaces to share memes. Tufte makes the parallel argument that the relationship between space and meaning-making is similar to the relationship between the acquisition/presentation of data and the "truth" that a person takes away from that presentation of data. Both arguments depend on the viewers' interpretation of spaces and data to gain a meaningful truth from both. Meme provides a bridge of understanding in showing what the meme creator thinks the data means to the audience that sees the meme creator's presentation in a given space.

Perhaps the biggest takeaway from Tufte's research related to memes is why people use memes as evidence for their arguments online. The simplification of a given position seems to be a strong reason for their continuous social media usage. Tufte's paradox would seem to be a rationale for their use. However, this streamlining of conversations via memes leaves out one of the critical factors in the online use of memes. It is also directly related to the memetic content creation process.

The production process for creating memes is quasi-collaborative. The meme creator is the primary force in the development, going through the memetic creative content production steps described in this chapter. The vital element to note as it relates to Tufte is that the community can tell the meme creator if the information they are presenting is significant and connects with them in some meaningful way. This process's quasi-collaborative nature is that the community or collective can directly impact future messages and memes the creator produces.

THE THERAPEUTIC CONSIDERATION

Dealing with the therapeutic angle of this part of the memetic communication process requires the therapist to dig into the creative process of crafting memes. A starting point for this conversation is to allow a meme creator to show their process of preparing their memetic content. I tend to think about these interactions as a type of "guided ethnographic study" (Tilton, 2012, 80) as a scholar and researcher in the field of social psychology.

It would seem that the participant observation model would be essentially the same paradigm in this level of engagement (Bogdewic, 1992). The active questioning that would typically be used in the guided ethnographic study should be used sparingly in a participant observation model. The result of any therapeutic interaction should be for a better understanding of individual behaviors and rituals instead of crafting a generalizable theory of human interactions.

Another point to consider is why meme creators are using specific tools. They may have a story about the first time that they used Imgur or Gimp. Therapists might find that this question leads to deeper conservation about people who helped the meme creator craft memes in the past or that the client is more comfortable talking about the abstract tools (as opposed to interactions with others).

The last of the therapeutic points to consider related to the meme production process is based on crafting messages and meaning within the meme. Three Ts find their way into most of the memetic content. **Takeaways** are what the meme creators hope is a meaningful message that the audience will remember, even if that message might be more chaotic (think about the deep-fried memes discussed earlier in this book). A more aesthetic point of this crafting process is the triggers within the meme. **Triggers** are visual or textual components of a meme that cause some sort of audience response, whether that is admiring the cuteness of kittens, laughing at a person's stupidity, or being shocked by a taboo subject. The last of the Ts is how the meme creator thinks they can move the community or collective in a particular direction. **Tracks** are the elements within memes that the creator uses to further an agenda, narrative, or social position. Hashtags presented in a meme, for example, can connect to a large movement online. Therapists need to recognize these three Ts to understand how the meme creators believe they connect with society and culture.

Works Cited

Askin, N., & Mauskapf, M. (2017). What Makes Popular Culture Popular? Product features and optimal differentiation in music. *American Sociological Review, 82*(5), 910-944.

Bebić, D., & Volarevic, M. (2018). Do not mess with a meme: the use of viral content in communicating politics. *Communication & Society, 31*(3), 43-56

Bogdewic, S. P. (1992). Participant Observation. In B. F. Crabtree & W. L. Miller (Eds.), *Research Methods for Primary Care (Volume 3): Doing qualitative research* (pg. 45–69). Sage Publications.

Castaño Díaz, C. M. (2013). Defining and Characterizing the Concept of Internet Meme. *Ces Psicología*, 6(2), 82-104.

Cleese, J. (2020). *Creativity: A short and cheerful guide.* Crown Imprint.

Coscia, M. (2014). Average is Boring: How similarity kills a meme's success. *Scientific Reports, 4*(1), 1-7.

Gehman, J., & Soublière, J. F. (2017). Cultural Entrepreneurship: From making culture to cultural making. *Innovation, 19*(1), 61-73.

Holm, N. H. (2017, July 14). Online Deadpan and the Comic Disposition. *Massey Research Online.* https://mro.massey.ac.nz/handle/10179/13374.

House Industries. (2017). *The Process is the Inspiration.* Watson-Guptill Publications.

Keats, J. (2013). *Forged: Why fakes are the great art of our age.* Oxford University Press.

Kleon, A. (2012). *Steal Like an Artist: 10 things nobody told you about being creative.* Workman Pub., Co.

Meredith, J. R., Shafer, S. M., & Mantel Jr, S. J. (2017). *Project Management: A strategic managerial approach.* John Wiley & Sons.

Meir, D. (2018). *Workflow: A practical guide to the creative process.* CRC Press.

Nissenbaum, A., & Shifman, L. (2018). Meme Templates as Expressive Repertoires in a Globalizing World: A cross-linguistic study. *Journal of Computer-Mediated Communication, 23*(5), 294-310.

Sugihartati, R. (2020). Youth Fans of Global Popular Culture: Between prosumer and free digital labourer. *Journal of Consumer Culture, 20*(3), 305-323.

Tilton, S. (2012). *First Year Students in a Foreign Fabric: A triangulation study on Facebook as a method of coping/adjustment* (dissertation). Ohio University, Athens, OH.

Toubia, O. (2017). The Summarization of Creative Content. *Columbia Business School Research Paper,* (pg. 17-86). https://papers.ssrn.com/sol3/papers.cfm?abstract_id=3020131

Townsend, P. (2019). *Creative States of Mind: Psychoanalysis and the artist's process.* Routledge.

CHAPTER 6:
INDUSTRIAL MEMES

It is fair to argue that memetic content is part of the broader cultural and creative industry that drives most of the institutions that we would consider part of any society. The visual, cultural, and textual layers of memes often use the content produced by creative professionals to communicate shared social experiences to the general public based on the public's experience with those artistic works. All forms of the cultural and creative content depend on media systems to distribute them.

Memes have a different level of engagement with the various members of society depending on what type of media the memes are transmitted through. Mass media tends to flatten a lot of the contextual meaning of memes, while more niche forms of media amplify the meme's context. The Internet is more dynamic when it comes to the level of message flattening that occurs when compared to other channels of communication. The speed associated with Internet transmission means that the content leaves the producer so quickly that others can remove all of the metaphorical fingerprints that would connect the content from the creator before the creator is even aware that they are being "erased" from their work.

The process of removing the artist from their work depends on how many traits the community members have in common (the more common traits shared between community members make it more likely that the individuality would be less pronounced in the final meme, thus making it harder to properly identify the original artist of the work) and the number of shared social experiences between members (like traits, common experiences among community members makes it hard to point on one person that is reflecting on that experience in the meme) related to the content in question. All of this analysis leads to a more profound question: what makes a meme viral? The idea of virality is better answered when addressing the concept of the "Meme Economy."

Besides talking about the systems outside of the ones that the meme creator can control, this chapter's focus will define an industry to study memetic content. Industries are vital in this discussion of memetic communication as they act as an external factor that influences memetic content creation. Beyond serving as the system that meme creators use to distribute their memes, industries play a role in shaping memetic content and how audiences read memes.

DEFINING CULTURAL INDUSTRY

The cultural industry concept comes from Theodor Adorno and Max Horkheimer's (1947) groundbreaking work, *Dialectic of Enlightenment*. That scholarship will be addressed in the conclusion of this chapter. An exploration of the connection between cultural industries and memetic communication requires a contemporary interpretation of these concepts. We need to start with a tangential means of addressing cultural industries from the 1970s before reaching the modern-day version of this term.

Paul M. Hirsch (1972) starts to hit on this tangent by addressing two points vital in understanding how memetic communication is part of the cultural industry. It is easy to note first that memetic communication allows for an end-product that is facilitated by organizations whose primary purpose is to create and distribute mediated works. Software suites like Adobe, social media services like Reddit, and communication companies like Verizon all play a role in allowing meme creators to craft their content based on the previous chapter's techniques. These powerful corporations control the mechanisms that are part of the memetic content creation process.

Hirsch's second point worth noting is the idea that cultural industries "entail relationships among a complex network of organizations which both facilitate and regulate the innovation process" (p. 640). This quote does not suggest that Adobe, Reddit, and Verizon are solely concerned with innovative memetic content, yet the innovations they produce will impact memetic culture. Verizon's (and all wireless phone companies') 5G service could allow for more video memes to be produced.

Moving the timeline to the 21st century, David Throsby (2004) denotes the idea that cultural industries have an impact on society and culture. Throsby uses the term impact in two ways: how a cultural work influences social institutions' economic interests and how industries change meme creators' ability to produce content. This book can not address the issues surrounding broad economic questions effectively. Therefore, we must put that part of the definition aside. That leaves with the second point.

At face value, Throsby and Hirsch are talking about similar topics. The difference is more nuanced. Throsby's is expressing how cultural industries form the foundation for movements or categories of memetic content. One of the problems this book addressed early on was that the categorization of memes rapidly changes. So we won't address that in this book because it would become out-dated as soon as the book was published. Throsby gives another tool to help readers of this work organize memetic content. Grouping memes by the means used to produce them is helpful to scholars as a way for noting the difference between memes and the significance of the layers within those memes. A more straightforward method is to sort memes by the platforms that initially publish them.

MASS MEDIA, SOCIAL MEDIA, AND NICHE MEDIA

In order to discuss the platforms that host memes means, we need a better understanding of how platforms help meme creators connect with their audience. This understanding gets to a critical discussion about the role of the media in this process. Media is one of the most misunderstood social institutions. It gets criticized often (the "mainstream media" being one of the more common insults) by those actively using the by-products of its system. At base level, the **media** is the combination of mediums (text, graphics, photography, audio, video, animation, etc.) that are placed together to transmit a message from one party (the sender) to another (the receiver) through a system that distributes (a channel) that combination of mediums (content).

Mass media is what people would typically associate with the term media. It is a social mechanism that allows for the transmission of most of the shows that we enjoy watching, music that we relish listening to, and other content that becomes part of our language that we use to express experiences with others. Content creators use the magic of the media to crystalize what it means to be human in the modern chaos of a changing society. The narratives that are part of these modes of expression will resonate with the audience when they feel like the content creators tell the stories of the audience member's daily life. Memes borrow the parts of those compelling narratives that the audience would recognize and use them as a shorthand for human conflicts, joys, and other emotions.

Social media acts as the primary means to send and receive memetic content. Unlike the one-to-many model that mass media content creators follow to craft their messages, meme creators on social media are more involved with their audiences through direct interactions. This level of connection between the audience and the creator allows the creator to appreciate the human condition and say something about it. All memes start in their creator's mind but must survive public scrutiny – to be mimicked, selected, and finally become part of the memetic communication lexicon. Once added to the community's daily use, it takes on an expanded role of developing its meaning through continued usage. Each community member's use of a meme means that the meme's contextual meaning evolves.

Niche media is functionally different from social and mass media as it seeks to cultivate a particular body of knowledge to share it with those interested in learning about the subject being covered by its content. Scholars in this field would argue that mass media's primary function is to act as an agent of socialization by defining cultural norms. The strength of social media is to develop communities that connect with aspects of the individual. Niche media (like podcasts, specialized newsfeeds, and paywalled websites) helps preserve experts' wisdom and the techniques related to a given technical subject rarely found on mass or social media platforms. About a decade ago, the term for those content creators working in niche media was *nanocelebrities* (Tilton, 2011).

All of the previously listed media types are part of the larger ecosystem that is the modern cultural industry. These various functional media constructions are useful to consider as part of the memetic communication process because the type of memes created on each platform are vastly different. Mass media memes likely speak to a generalizable part of the human condition that resonates with a wide breadth of the population. Memes developed on social media sites will reflect the spirit of that particular community. Niche memes build their novelty on a creative view of the jargon, skills, and experiences that only the subject's practitioners would have familiarity with. These various media systems' functions allow content creators to express something that is happening in society and let the audience determine the truthfulness of those expressions.

DISTILLING SOCIETY'S SENSIBILITIES INTO MEMETIC CONTENT

To address how the audience determines the truthfulness of a given meme's central message means that we need to discuss how meme creators can express social truths within the meme. Meme creators are often members of the community or collective in which they are sharing their content. This connection with the community or collective means that they can synthesize a social norm, topic, or issue that the memetic structure is addressing. Consider the "Ice Bucket Challenge." The memetic aspects of the challenge allowed individuals and communities to put a local twist on the activity that defines the community / individual and then embed it within the meme. Bill Gates made a slightly nerdy twist to it by building a device to pour the ice water on his head. Macklemore turned it into a music video. Jimmy Fallon invited his guests, band (The Roots), and announcer to perform the challenge in the style of his late-night show. These three examples show how memes allow for the ability to introduce unique aesthetics into these digital works.

Shifman's four phases of memetic development would indicate that in order for a meme to reach the hypermemetic (read as mass popularity) stage, it needs to be selected by the community and shared with others (the selection process). Memes are partly a "Mad Libs" story structure wrapped in the mediated elements to be pleasing to the community and therefore be selected for wide sharing. Both memes and Mad Libs' build a collective sense of the community's narrative by allowing everybody to participate in the creation process. Granted, memes tend to be more focused in their messaging, as one person is responsible for an individual meme. However, the spectrum of memes has this sense of absurdity as the community can use the medium in whatever creative ways they choose.

145

The term **sensibilities** is, perhaps, a more constructive way to think about this encapsulation. Successful memes do not specifically have to reflect the standard actions, beliefs, values, and attitudes of community members but tend to reflect on the way "others" act, what they should believe, what values they should have, and the attitudes they should express. "Others" refers to the imagined social order that includes the meme viewer and its creator. Memes can express an idealized representation of reality or air of grievances or even be the voice in a person's head looking for an audience. Despite its vague definitions and conceptualizations, culture is still the means to train people to socialize. Cultural industries are built as a form of control, which is the opposite of the other industry that drives memetic content.

DEFINING CREATIVE INDUSTRY

Creative industries are the modern version of the cultural industry, as they focus on the individual's statement to society, conveyed by their aesthetic decisions and their branding of themselves. These industries are more about leaving an impact on other people's taste and style. One of the best-known examples of a creative industry would be Andy Warhol's Factory. The Factory was the nickname for Warhol's New York City studio as it seemed to fit the place's mood. It was an assembly line for all sorts of creative works; silkscreening canvases, filming a short movie, and other creative endeavors were crafted by a regular cast of artists better known as his "superstars" (Watson, 2003).

There are two reasons that Warhol's Factory works as a model for understanding creative industries. Warhol's quote, "In the future, everyone will be world-famous for 15 minutes," speaks to the quick-shifting nature of the public's attention span and the broadness of the focus of media audiences. In the moment of writing this book, a sea shanty, Nathan Evans' version of "The Wellerman," was placed on two of the Billboard charts (Global 200 and Global Excluding U.S.) and several international charts (Canada, Germany, Ireland, Netherlands, New Zealand, Sweden, and the United Kingdom). It is fair to place ShantyTok in this discussion of creative industries as it represents Warhol's quote and the nature of creative industries. TikTok, as a cultural industry, drove the distribution of the song, but Nathan Evans was a creative industry within the system and used that distribution to find popularity and some financial success by working with other talented individuals on the site to create a remix of the original song that became popular worldwide. It is also fair to predict the ShantyTok will wane in popularity by the time this book is published (or way before this book is published depending on the editing process that modern books take).

The second reason to consider Warhol's Factory when discussing creative industries is the Factory's multimodal nature. Creative industries are not stuck on one medium or one mode of expression. Instead, creative industries understand what is popular and adapt their creativity to the medium of accessibility. The medium of accessibility simply refers to a creative industry using a medium that will allow their message and content to spread the farthest and the fastest. TikTok videos were the medium of accessibility that allowed Evans to get his music in front of a critical mass of people, thus guaranteeing the song's success. Memes are another medium of accessibility due to their portability and ease of sharing across social media platforms.

ARE MEMES INTELLECTUAL PROPERTIES?

A logical extension of this creative industry analysis should consider the relationship between memes and the creative industries that produce them. Beyond being one of the potential end-products of those creative industries, these digital works could be considered stand-alone intellectual properties that are "independent" from the original context and popular cultural content (e.g., movies, graphic novels, and video games) that helped develop the final product of the meme.

To address this question of intellectual property, we should consider how much of the meme is a unique expression crafted by the meme creator alone. Originality is often a criterion posed in copyright claims about popular culture work. Is the one note that distinguishes the melodies of Ice, Ice Baby and Under Pressure enough to make them separate intellectual properties (Grelecki, 2005)? For this book, we will not worry about the legal definitions of intellectual properties. Some legal scholars have waxed philosophical about these judicial points for years (Samuelson, 1985; Coombe, 1998; Fitzpatrick & DiLullo, 2005; Johnson, 2013; Landers, 2020). Instead, we will address the concept of **intellectual properties** as any work of media that expresses its creator's thoughts about how their beliefs, values, attitudes, and behaviors relate to social and cultural influences and subjects and expressing those thoughts in a mediated format.

The discussion about intellectual properties is beneficial from a scholarly perspective because memes can be examined as stand-alone cultural expressions and an individual's creative output. Understanding memes as cultural expressions means that people use this format to present a discrete snapshot of a representation of any community topic (using a meme to remind people about the importance of voting), spotlight key points related to an issue or debate (as in most political memes), or even highlight an important date or event (election day memes). For example, political movements like the Arab Spring were driven by memetic communication (Saideman, 2012). This power to drive people to act is partly why we need to discuss the literal and figurative nature of the "Meme Economy."

THE MEME ECONOMY

The idea of the "Meme Economy" is itself a memetic artifact and the means to explain the value of memes as social and cultural artifacts. The concept was part of the Reddit culture beginning around 2016. It was originally a way to make fun of taking memes too seriously and poking fun at financial journalism's seriousness. The subreddit /r/MemeEconomy was the consolidation of memes that referred to this concept (like "Mad Karma with Jim Cramer" and the NASDANQ) and showed what the community thought was popular and worth other people's attention. The ultimate by-product of this concept was *Meme Insider*, a magazine devoted to "trading memes" (Bateman, 2017). It can be challenging to treat such an expression as sincere. The purpose of understanding this concept is more about finding popular memes, as opposed to determining the seriousness of such an idea of trading memes. The popularity of memes speaks to two prominent trends within the Meme Economy concept.

One of the main ideas that the Meme Economy shines a light on is that when memes become too popular, they lose their novelty. Losing a meme's novelty means that the content is no longer a creative expression of the meme creator's viewpoint of a given topic or issue. It becomes noise online. Novelty is what draws attention. This idea calls back Gestalt theory, and precisely

149

the maxim of habituation. Habituation refers to the concept that the mind protects itself from overstimulation and unnecessary pictures by ignoring visual stimuli that are a part of a person's everyday, habitual activities. Habituation occurs when we stop paying attention to something. Simply put, we may have seen it so much that we no longer notice it. For the Meme Economy, overexposed memes lose value.

The second trend to consider is that memes might become popular based on the layers within the meme. For example, during a health crisis, stocks' value in the medical sector tend to rise (Boswijk, Hommes, & Manzan, 2007). In the Meme Economy, if a character like Spongebob has a movie coming out, more Spongebob memes will appear. This trend is partly due to the mere exposure effect in action (people will continue to use images and sounds from the shows, movies, and other mediated work that they enjoy), where the introduction of a new mediated work will re-engage the community to use the symbols of that show, movie, book, video game, or soundtrack (Tilton, 2019).

Another way to view the Meme Economy concept is that those who participated in these simulations of the stock market found that their training has a real-world impact. The clearest example of this connection is the "GameStonk" event. GameStonk refers to GameStop and a memetic representation of the Meme Economy, the Stonk. Redditers on the r/WallStreetBets used their memetic training to push a stock ("GameStop") that investors thought would lose money. Those Reddit investors pushed the stock value more than 1,000% over several days (Roche, 2021).

Figure 13: The Stonk memetic artifact, a surrealistic representation that originally referred to making bad financial decisions and evolved to a symbol of the GameStonk Redditors. (Holly McCoy)

The memetic connection is that most of the investors were buying the stock not because they thought GameStop was a sound economic property, but because they were performing a memetic action as a strike against Wall Street and the hedge fund managers that the Redditers believe were harming America (Gara, 2021). The "Stonks" memetic artifact became more than a message crystallized in an image. It became a symbol that the GameStonk Redditers rallied behind, helping send the GameStop stock price (in the words of the GameStonk supporters) "to the moon." It is fair to argue that the GameStonk meme was viral in the sense that the Stonk meme was actively part of online communication and that people were performing the memetic action of buying GameStop stock. Virality occurs in both of the industries we discussed in this chapter.

VIRALITY OF MEMES IN THE CULTURAL AND CREATIVE INDUSTRIES

One of the points of confusion that occurs when discussing memetic content is the amount of overlap with viral content. A meme itself is not necessarily viral in nature. Creating a meme does not guarantee that everybody will be willing to share that work. Communities and collectives act as a gatekeeper that can prevent its ability to spread to the general public. It must go through Shifman's "Four Phases of Memetic Works" to break past the boundaries of the community or collective.

There tend to be three driving forces that will increase the likelihood that a meme goes viral once the work has enough momentum to leave a given community or collective: the viral nature of memetic artifacts comes from reaching a critical mass of awareness, a low cultural capital needed to understand the artifact, and sometimes, the ease of performability to the memetic artifact. All of these factors work in tandem to amplify both the messaging within the meme and the meme's exposure to the general public. Both cultural and creative industries play a part in producing viral content.

We have discussed both cultural capital and memetic performances in previous chapters. The **critical mass of awareness** is the concept we need to dig into a little more detail as it is more than an abstract point that a meme hits. It is the moment in which an average person is more likely than not to recognize a specific version of a meme. It's the high point that people are more likely to see the same layers form a perfect replica of a digital work on two or more social media nodes. Cultural industries are built to spread the exact copy of memes with minimal effort. People in the creative industries try to hit this point by finding what is popular and adapting their content to have some of the characteristics of other viral works.

Repurposing cultural capital is the strength of the creative industries. They depend on content creators finding the narratives in other mediated work to touch on the stories that speak to others' experiences. Henry Jenkins hit on this idea back in 1992 with his book *Textual Poachers*. Meme creators, like the creators Jenkins was referring to, depend on a participatory culture mindset like artists and communicators to go beyond the media's mere consumption. Those creators "become active participants in the construction and circulation of textual meanings" (Jenkins, 1992, 24) in order to create new cultural materials for society and apply those narratives happening in fictional works to real-world situations. Jenkins is using fan fiction as his paradigm for this action. Meme creators are doing the same thing, just creating memes instead of writing.

Memetic performances occur because both cultural and creative industries are working together to give a platform for these offerings. The cultural side of the equation will often consider how users interact with their tools to add innovations to those tools. The most obvious example of a cultural industry making it easier to spread memetic performance is when Twitter made hashtags embedded links on their site. When people type in an octothorpe[1] (#) followed by letters and numbers, a link is created using those letters and numbers as a search term on Twitter. Hashtags like #WholesomeMemes, #TwitterCrush, and #WW3 (short for World War 3) will each link to a separate page on Twitter that has a feed of content that acts as an archive of the community's memes and postings where the poster uses that hashtag in their tweet.

This addition to Twitter functionally gave users the ability to develop, in the words of Axel Bruns and Jean Burgess, an "ad hoc publics" that allows for a public sphere of engagement around that term (Bruns & Burgess, 2011). Creative industries use those

---

[1]Yes, (1) that is the real name for the hashtag symbol, (2) it is a cool name for that symbol, and (3) you will forget that name.

public spheres to address more people connected to the sphere and display their creative works within that communal bubble. A fair example of this concept came from 2020 during their #MetT-winning campaign. The Met Twinning was a response to both the pandemic and promoting The Met. The hashtag was used by both Twitter and Instagram to have people recreate famous works of art at home. One post had a girl wearing a light blue head covering, a gold-colored blanket and a pearl clip-on earring to recreate Johannes Vermeer's famous painting "Girl with a Pearl Earring." Antioch Austin College posted a photo of a man wearing an overcoat and bowler hat with an apple in front of his face. This photo recreated Rene Magritte's "The Son of Man." This hashtag formed an ad hoc public of both fans of arts and supporters of the Metropolitan Museum of Art.

The last significant difference between memetic artifacts and viral content focuses on the audience's relationship to both works. Memetic artifacts depend on users applying the remixing, selecting, and hypermemetic phases of Shifman's Four Phases of Memetic Works to keep the meme alive. Viral content simply needs the audience to share the work without remixing for the content to be viral. It is a stand-alone cultural artifact with no need for the community or collective to add additional layers on top of it to be successful.

ADORNO & HORKHEIMER'S MEMETIC CULTURAL INDUSTRY

We should end where we began this chapter and talk about how Theodor Adorno and Max Horkheimer viewed the role of culture in society. One of the more groundbreaking arguments Adorno and Horkheimer made in *Dialectic of Enlightenment* was that humans depend on the freedom to express their thoughts to others, a creative outlet for those expressions, and a feeling of genuine happiness based on acceptance and understanding to fulfill their basic psychological needs. Mass-produced culture robs people of those three things. They echo the points raised by Neil Postman (2006) in *Amusing Ourselves to Death* as "the media" invites the general public to select their entertainment and information based on the paths of least resistance and least objection. Easy access to content can make us passive consumers of the media, making us passive citizens.

Memes begin to counter that passivity, as there are multiple phases that people can participate in and engage, via the conversations happening online. As described before, there are low barriers to participation in this form of communication. MySpace, Friendster, Facebook, Twitter, Instagram, SnapChat, and any other service that can share content also created the user interfaces that allowed for the creation of new content. Most of that content was textual at first, then slowly adding frames on pictures or enhancing media with additional information was introduced, becoming the foundation of memetic creation. People began to see the Internet as a place they could use to engage with creative forms of expression, like memes.

It is this freedom of expression online (while limited to the desires and whims of the companies that own the various platforms) that allows people to reach a point of enlightenment based on the beliefs, values, attitudes, and behaviors grounded in the rituals, philosophies, and other institutional narratives spread via socialization. **Institutional narratives** refer to any of the underlying stories associated with government organizations and other organizing forces in society. How we define patriotism is an institutional narrative, for example. People will respond to those societal forces and challenge them if given the tools to think critically about them. Adorno & Horkheimer calls this process engaging with **critical social theory**.

Stepping away from the broad implications of critical social theory means that we can examine how a meme creator or meme user employs this process. At a base level, memes allow both creators and users to engage with daily life mythologies. Memes can point to the absurdity of human behavior (as shown in the Fail Blog section of the meme site cheezburger.com), the expressive nature of humans (as demonstrated by the Wojak series of memes), offer advice/wisdom (as represented by so called "Advice Animal Image Macro" category of memes, which includes Advice Dog, Confession Bear, Office Cat, and others), and stereotypes of human behavior (as displayed in the human "Internet Character" memes by Scumbag Steve, Robbie Rotten, and Hide the Pain Harold). Examining memes as a series of layers can help break that narrative chain.

Thoughtfully examining memes addresses the final concern raised by both Adorno & Horkheimer related to this book. The focus on turning all forms of mediated works into commodities as part of the cultural industries' hyper-commercialization of all aspects of life means that all pieces are determined by value alone. Critiquing memes fights the reduction of memes as mere economic tools designed to promote organizational agendas, corporations' bottom-lines, or governments' policies. People injecting their views into these forms forces community members to have serious conversations about the impact of culture (e.g., using memes to present counter-arguments about how violence in video games promotes violence in society), societal issues (e.g., the Black Lives Matter social movement), and the state of the world in general.

THE THERAPEUTIC CONSIDERATION

Of the five parts of the memetic definition, showing a client how they connect with the cultural and creative industries of memetic content can be tricky. Most of the time, clients are passively sharing the work with others without considering the underlying process used to create the meme. Forgetting that memes were created by someone removes the contributions of the meme creator, thus takes power and agency away from the creator and drives it back to social institutions and forces that shape society. Meme creators are interconnected with both industries in that they depend on the tools provided by cultural industries and the content crafted by the creative industries to make memes. It seems fair when acknowledging those factors to take a social-psychological approach to the therapeutic practice.

A good icebreaker to begin discussing cultural industries would be, "what software and sites do you use to craft and post your memes?" User interfaces, algorithms, and the other mechanisms that define the software and services also become the connection points that meme creators have with the rest of the world. The Adobe paradigm of media-authoring applications (like Photoshop and InDesign) allows meme creators to see the screen as a canvas to layer content to craft a completed work (Manovich, 2013). Understanding these tools can help a clinician approach how the client sees themselves connected with the world.

Questions such as, "who or what influences memes that you create?" or "what about this person's style do you like to use in your work?" can also aid the discussion. Asking questions of this nature gets shorter answers. A person might give one or two names of their influences but provide brief responses to the why. Those reflective analyses are brief, as it can be hard to denote the abstract concept that speaks to a client (Grushka, 2005). It is not unusual to hear answers like "it pops," "it speaks to me," "it's eye-catching," and other similar statements without a more explicit rationale. A great follow-up question can be "who else or what other memes shared that same quality of (it pops, it speaks to me, it's eye-catching, etc.)?" Those types of follow-ups might lead to a narrative breakthrough about the client's influences and internal motivations.

Those clients who do not create memes are better served by approaching the cultural industries side of the equation. Questions like "what sites do you find have the memes you most often share" will give the client an avenue to think about why those sites have the memes that the client likes the most. This conversation might also lead to a discussion about the communities and collectives that share the client's beliefs and values.

These questions help the client think about how they connect the client and show that they are part of the memetic content creation process. They create memes, share memes, or comment on memes. At the base level, the superstructure of the Internet is required to send and receive content. The Internet also acts as the connective thread linking the various industries described in this chapter. In the broadest sense, the chapter focuses on how we are all connected through online communication.

Works Cited

Adorno, T. W., & Horkheimer, M. (1997). *Dialectic of Enlightenment (Vol. 15).* Verso.

Bateman, O.L. (2017). *Redditors Made 'Meme Insider,' a Completely Insane Magazine About Memes.* Retrieved February 12, 2021, from https://www.vice.com/en/article/53jgdb/redditors-made-meme-insider-a-completely-insane-magazine-about-memes

Boswijk, H. P., Hommes, C. H., & Manzan, S. (2007). Behavioral Heterogeneity in Stock Prices. *Journal of Economic Dynamics and Control, 31*(6), 1938-1970.

Bruns, A., & Burgess, J. (2011). *The Use of Twitter Hashtags in the Formation of Ad Hoc Publics.* In Proceedings of the 6th European consortium for political research (ECPR) general conference 2011 (pp. 1-9). The European Consortium for Political Research (ECPR).

Coombe, R. J. (1998). *The Cultural Life of Intellectual Properties: Authorship, appropriation, and the law.* Duke University Press.

Fitzpatrick, W. M., & DiLullo, S. A. (2005). Strategic Alliances and the Management of Intellectual Properties: The art of the contract. *SAM Advanced Management Journal, 70*(3), 38-45.

Gara, A. (2021). *The Hedge Fund Genius Who Started GameStop's 4,800% Rally Now Calls It "Unnatural, Insane, And Dangerous."* Retrieved February 11, 2021, from https://www.forbes.com/sites/antoinegara/2021/01/26/the-hedge-fund-genius-who-started-gamestops-4800-rally-now-calls-it-unnatural-insane-and-dangerous/?sh=423149e8303b

Grelecki, R. C. (2005). Can Law and Economics Bring the Funk... or Efficiency: A law and economics analysis of digital sampling. *Florida State University Law Review, 33*, 297-330.

Grushka, K. (2005). Artists as Reflective Self-learners and Cultural Communicators: An exploration of the qualitative aesthetic dimension of knowing self through reflective practice in art-making. *Reflective Practice, 6*(3), 353-366.

Hirsch, P. (1972). Processing Fads and Fashions: An organization-set analysis of cultural industry systems. *American Journal of Sociology, 77*(4), 639-659. Retrieved February 1, 2021, from http://www.jstor.org/stable/2776751

Jenkins, H. (2012). *Textual Poachers: Television fans and participatory culture.* Routledge.

Johnson, D. (2013). *Media Franchising: Creative license and collaboration in the culture industries (Vol. 11).* NYU Press.

Landers, A. L. (2020). Hyperreal: Law and the interpretation of visual media. *Kentucky Law Journal, 109*(1), 1-64.

Manovich, L. (2013). *Software Takes Command (Vol. 5).* A&C Black.

Postman, N. (2006). *Amusing Ourselves to Death: Public discourse in the age of show business.* Penguin.

Roche, C. (2021). *Three Things I Think I Think – GAMESTONK!* Retrieved February 11, 2021, from https://www.pragcap.com/three-things-i-think-i-think-gamestonk/

Samuelson, P. (1985). Creating a New Kind of Intellectual Property: Applying the lessons of the chip law to computer programs. *Minnesota Law Review, 70*, 471-532.

Saideman, S. M. (2012). When Conflict Spreads: Arab Spring and the limits of diffusion. *International Interactions, 38*(5), 713-722.

Throsby, D. (2004). Assessing the Impacts of a Cultural Industry. *The Journal of Arts Management, Law, and Society, 34*(3), 188-204.

Tilton, S. (2019). Songs of the Ritos: The psychology of the music within the Legend of Zelda series. In Anthony Bean's (ed.) *The Psychology of Zelda: Linking our world to the Legend of Zelda series,* 171-190, Smart Pop Books.

Watson, S. (2003). *Factory Made: Warhol and the sixties.* Pantheon Books.

CHAPTER 7: MEMES AS A COMMUNICATIVE ACT

THOMAS WESTON ADAMS III

In the past, the effects of media were experienced more gradually, allowing the individual and society to absorb and cushion their impact to some degree. Today, in the electronic age of instantaneous communication, I believe that our survival, and at the very least our comfort and happiness, is predicated on understanding the nature of our new environment, because unlike previous environmental changes, the electric media constitute a total and near-instantaneous transformation of culture, values and attitudes. This upheaval generates great pain and identity loss, which can be ameliorated only through a conscious awareness of its dynamics. If we understand the revolutionary transformations caused by new media, we can anticipate and control them; but if we continue in our self-induced subliminal trance, we will be their slaves.

Because of today's terrific speed-up of information moving, we have a chance to apprehend, predict and influence the environmental forces shaping us – and thus win back control of our own destinies.

These are the words of Marshall McLuhan, famed communication theorist. He uttered these words during a *Playboy Magazine* interview, and when his "today" was referring to the year 1969 (Norden, 1969). McLuhan describes our inability to grasp the effects of media as "a syndrome whereby man remains as unaware of the psychic and social effects of his new technology as a fish of the water it swims in. As a result, precisely at the point where a new media-induced environment becomes all pervasive... it also becomes invisible." As memetic communication becomes pervasive in our world, we in this chapter of *Meme Life* endeavor to expose, illuminate, elucidate, reveal the workings of memes as a way of communicating — as a medium.

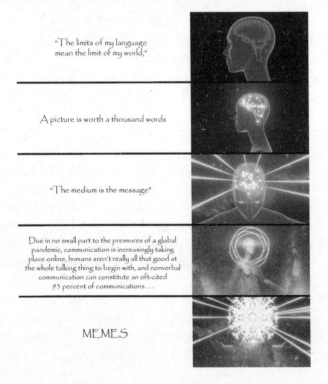

Figure 14: An example of a Galaxy Brain meme that explains memetic content.

TRADITIONAL DEFINITIONS/UNDERSTANDINGS OF COMMUNICATION AND HOW MEMES FIT

Consider how communication is introduced to those studying it for the first time. Communication — it's a "complex process through which people produce, interpret, and coordinate messages to create shared meanings, achieve social goals, manage their personal identities, and carry out their relationships" (Verderber & MacGeorge, 2015, 4). This definition implies that communication is ongoing and dynamic (involving generation, creation, dissemination, reception, engagement, and management). Communication takes place in systems consisting of interrelated parts that affect one another (Wood, 2016, 10). Communication involves interaction. It employs the use of symbols[2]. It involves creation and interpretation, sending and receiving. Communication is an active process. It involves multiple layers of encoded messages, verbal(linguistic)/ nonverbal (nonlinguistic) elements, and has content and relational dimensions. It is influenced by the environment, culture, and social factors. It's the process of managing messages to create shared meaning. Communication is the stuff of life and the way by which we live — better put, it's the seeing, the making, and the doing (Eberly, 2000). Now let us compare this understanding of communication to the definition of memes from the first chapter.

Memes are active, multilayered communication constructions which are influenced by social factors and represent a mode of individual expression, in which meaning-making is controlled by both a community who understands that the whole of the work is greater than the sum of its parts and a collective that places creative

---

[2]Symbols are ambiguous, arbitrary, abstract.

content into some part of the broader cultural industry embedded in society.

The similarities between these definitions and therefore between these phenomena are undeniable. Memes are perfectly situated to be discussed in terms of communication for a number of reasons. It might seem obvious that memes are, in fact and on its face, communication proper. But it is in the exploration of how memes fit the bill that makes this chapter worthwhile. Memes have become woven into the fabric of our lives, but that fabric is and always has been communication. Memes are an accepted coin of the realm and are also generative of what constitutes *koina* (in the Aristotelian sense). For this chapter's discussion, let's consider memes as communication in a manner consistent with (oftentimes literal) textbook treatments of the matter.

Introductory communication and interpersonal relationships classes and corresponding texts often break down the curriculum along familiar lines, such as:

1. culture,

2. perception,

3. language/verbal,

4. body language/nonverbal,

5. listening,

6. emotions,

7. close/intimate relationships,

8. friendships,

9. conflict,

10. climate,

11. individuals vs. groups,

12. organizations,

13. leadership,

14. problem solving,

15. public communication,

16. mass media,

17. social media,

18. and the like[3].

Memes can be used to help explain each of these areas of introductory communication class, but we're going to work the other way around. If we come to a better understanding of communication, it'll be easier to see how mimetic communication works. Traditionally, social media or the very rare mention of memes, is tacked to the end of chapters or added into boxes or side notes in official university-level reading materials. Here, in *Meme Life* — it's one of the guiding principles.

---

[3]Memes are found in cultures around the world. They vary culture to culture. Memes help us make our perceptions clear to others and also help us to see things more clearly or in a different context. Memes integrate linguistic communication and nonverbal or image or video based information into a multilayered artifact. Memes highlight the importance of listening and clearly demonstrate the pitfalls of communication incompetence. Memes, like tweets, can distill emotions into a form that makes it easier or even more comfortable to communicate vulnerability. In memes, close relationships have another tool in their toolbox with which they can build a stronger bond. Memes can also make clear or at times oversimplify contentious moments. Memes can also demonstrate and create positive or negative communication climates. Memes can be shared among individuals or groups, and the different types of groups can have different responses and uses for memes (consider at home vs at school vs at work). We saw a President govern by tweet for four years, and regardless of any critiques of his leadership, President Trump unquestionably used the medium to great influence. Memes can be used to project leadership, can assist in solving problems, can be made public or kept private and interpersonal, are routinely found in mass media discourse, and are the clear coin of the realm on social media.

THE FULFILLMENT OF NEEDS

Communication, at its most fundamental, a key characteristic of human existence, can be seen as fulfilling several basic needs (physical, instrumental/practical, relational, identity).

PHYSICAL NEEDS

Humans, inherently social creatures, require communication for survival. There are strong ties between health, well-being, and communication. Long before the pandemic scholars knew that prolonged isolation could severely damage a human (Williams & Zadro, 2001), that individuals with good interpersonal communication skills are better able to adapt to stress and have less depression and anxiety (Hargie, 2011), and that the absence of communication can be linked to health problems. Greene, Derlega, & Mathews (2006) found that spouses of suicide or accidental death victims who did not communicate about the death with their friends were more likely to have health problems such as weight change and headaches than those who did talk with friends.

There's a stirring set of textbook examples used in courses that teach this content. Countless tales of subversive communication among detained or incarcerated individuals appear in literature and storytelling. Even former US Senator and Presidential nominee, the late John McCain, has been the direct subject of lessons illustrating communication fulfilling our most basic physical needs — communication allowing us to keep a grip on life and one's place in it. There's value in just being able to exchange words with another human.

Connected or happily partnered individuals with robust social relationships even live longer4 as they are at lower risk of coronary disease, obesity, hypertension; whereas divorced or widowed individuals experience higher rates of hospitalization due to mental illness. Happily partnered individuals see lower rates of "pneumonia, surgery, and cancer" (Adler, 2015, 6). Moveover, these relationships can even create a form of resilience observable at the stress hormone level — individuals with strong social bonds see fewer stress- related hospitalizations and deaths (McGonigle, 2013).

INSTRUMENTAL NEEDS

Instrumental/practical needs are another obvious set of needs met via communication. It's functional communication that serves a clear/bounded purpose. Consider workplace emails and announcements. Instructions or directions or requests make clear the functional nature of communication in our everyday lives. Syllabi and other student-oriented discourse increasingly incorporate memes in an obvious effort to increase relevance and promote engagement. In this post-pandemic world, keeping abreast of current regulations and restrictions is part and parcel of daily life.

IDENTITY AND SOCIAL/RELATIONAL NEEDS

Just as a meme can be used to help fulfill practical or functional needs, that same content can be used to establish one's identity or or foster relationships with others.

---

4 3.7 years longer (Adler, 2021, 6)

PEOPLE WITH VACCINE CARDS BE LIKE

Figure 15: An example of a meme that establishes identity. (Holly McCoy)

Our identity needs are met via communication — the primary way we understand and define ourselves and also how we project that understanding/definition.

The listicle as shareable content has itself become a meme. 43 memes only people who X during Y will understand might seem all too familiar (Golder, 2018). Memes or references to memetic content can be used as dating profiles or LinkedIn/resume content. Apps/software/technologies intimately tied to one's identity, like the popular Bitmoji (or even Snapchat itself), allow for individuals to merge their own likenesses with the meme world.

Perhaps most obviously, communication works toward the fulfillment of social/relational needs. The virtual or face-to-face hugs, kisses, birthday wishes, communication is the stuff of relationships (forming and fostering). Memes now fulfill numerous social/relational functions and, ultimately, needs.

MEMES FUNCTION AS INTERPERSONAL/ RELATIONAL COMMUNICATION

Self-disclosure, a core component of identity creation, connects identity needs with relational or social needs. It's how we define ourselves for ourselves and to others. The website and corresponding book series, *Post Secret*, or the app *Whisper*, or even older sites like *LiveJournal*, have long demonstrated the desire or market demand for places individuals can share secrets or other personal information in a safe or, rather, more comfortable manner. Because memes can typically laugh or shrug off criticism due to a reserved air of lightness, memes present a potentially desirable avenue for sharing personal information on social media — they provide cover. Individuals are able to encode messages in memes more carefully or hide behind the protection of a shared meme—something they themselves didn't create.

TRADITIONAL MODELS OF COMMUNICATION AND HOW THEY MEME

Explaining communication has undergone some changes over the years. Early communication models viewed it solely as information transfer (and frequently, this transfer was unidirectional). Later models moved to include listener or audience feedback, thus enabling an interactive understanding of communication. It also took quite some time for our models to acknowledge nonverbal communication as a natural part of communication.

One helpful way to learn about accepted understandings of communication is to become familiar with the modeling of communication. At its most basic, communication involves:

1. a sender,

2. a receiver,

3. a message,

4. the processes of encoding and decoding the message in question,

5. and a manner by/through which the message is sent.

Basic communication models often incorporate noise, internal or external elements that get in the way of a message being sent or received. We might also include context, environment, or cultural elements in the model. The words channel or medium might also appear as a way to demarcate the manner of message transmission. One-way communication channels seek to broadcast information, while two-way communication channels seek interaction/feedback as part of the process.

Today, communication courses move quickly to models that incorporate real-time (as compared to turn-taking) interactivity or feedback. Most communication scholars consider all parties as simultaneous senders/receivers, typically culminating in what communication professionals call the **transactional model of communication**. Transactional models of communication recognize the pervasive nature of communication and embrace the ongoing or always moving.

The basic, widely accepted models of communication are helpful in our effort to understand memes as communication. But, it's important to note that scholars are currently struggling to conceptualize and model the myriad forms of mediated communication present in our lives. Electronic communication, social media, and the internet introduce apparent complexity to the systems and present significant difficulty to those attempting to model contemporary communication.

How should our models reflect the inclusion of the internet? Scholars continue to struggle with this question.

Communication shared online isn't going to be the same as words exchanged face-to-face alone in a room. Interpersonal communication is distinct from mass or public communication, and public tweets or Insta-stories are distinct from private messages. Another distinction is between communication that is a two-way dialogue between specific people vs. communication that is a one-way broadcast for a given audience. We must consider these distinctions to understand what response the receiver will give based on the method of communication. Pushing a focus on the expectation of a response from the sender, French and Bodorova (2017) attempt to illuminate a third way in which they consider "anticipated response and imagined responsive audience as key parameters of masspersonal communication because they pave the way for a communicative relationship and message exchange between senders and receivers" (305). Memes can walk the line between mediated interpersonal communication, public communication, and something communication scholars have labeled **masspersonal communication** (communication that can reach large audiences while forging and fostering personal or seemingly personal connections).

Surely memes are interactive, but they are fully realized when viewed as transactional, intentional/unintentional, irreversible, and unrepeatable.

CORE QUALITIES OF COMMUNICATION

Jumping off with insights from the models of communication, we can isolate other basic principles of communication. First, communication is transactional. Communication is a dynamic process that the participants create through their interactions with one another. This process, of course, is detailed in previous chapters related to memes and their life cycle. There's a reason why memes fall flat when teachers or office managers use them in their syllabi or email reminders. Memes are participatory and constructed with a democratic spirit. At their core, they embrace, acknowledge, or even require always already transactional nature of communication.

Communication can be both intentional and unintentional. While meme creation is intentional to some degree, memes can contain multitudes - myriad messages live within memes, and many of those messages may have been initially unintentional. Communication is irreversible; it is impossible to "unreceive" a message, once said or done or posted. The overwhelming looming presence of the Internet in the world further elucidates the fleeting nature, yet also the deceptively permanent nature of online posts.

Once memes are out there — they can't be taken back. It's very difficult or near impossible to disappear a meme from the annals of the Internet. We're primed to recall the words of friends or enemies of the past. Praise or disparagement may ring in our ears well beyond its heyday. Even corrections in media have a tough time finding their way into the conversation — even in the days where print media ruled the stage, corrections would appear in a later edition, typically on a page buried deep in the publication. When it comes to communication — you might apologize, but no takebacks[5].

A person or publication may revise a statement or delete a tweet, making it very difficult to discern the original version or form, but when it comes to the Internet, it's very likely always possible that some version will survive. Messaging apps allow for messages to be unsent or removed, but many times this is only possible for a message recently shared. Facebook Messenger, for example, leaves a note informing the other members of the chat that a message has been removed. Instagram, on the other hand, allows for messages to be unsent without informing other parties. Just as there are no takebacks — also, there are no mulligans. Communication is unrepeatable. The same words and behavior are different each time they are spoken or performed.

This central tenet of communication is particularly poignant for a discussion of *Meme Life* as it is in the nature of memetic communication to repeat — memes by definition are imminently repeatable. But each repetition has a different sender, a different audience, different timing, a different situation into which it interjects. It's this core principle of communication that powers the ancient Hera-

---

[5]Consider the saga of Pepe the Frog — in which the creator ultimately kills of the character in the comic strip in an effort to fight the unsanctioned use of the character by right wing extremists and white supremacists. Even after Pepe's death as a character in the comic, and long after much attention was called to the problematic (to say the least) use of his image, Pepe routinely shows up in online discourse and in real world protests in 2020 and 2021, even in Hong Kong. This miniature case study serves as instructive for each of the communication misconceptions listed above.(Source: https://knowyourmeme.com/memes/pepe-the-frog)

clitus' claim that a man, or in our cases a meme, "cannot step into the same river twice" (Dresser, 2019).

CONTENT / RELATIONAL

Communication has a content dimension and a relational dimension. The content dimension involves the information being explicitly discussed, while the relational dimension expresses how you feel about the other person or how the person receiving the message relates to the content of the message on an emotional level. In every meme there is the straightforward content, the individual components and their orientation/juxtaposition/layering/sequencing, but then there are the resulting feelings — the subjective emotional responses to everything contained and communicated therein. When I see the meme it's just a guy I don't know (same as a stock image) and a caption. When my uncle sees the meme I made about him, "It just hit different." (Mulaney, 2019).

COMMUNICATION COMPETENCE, MESSAGE RECEPTION, AND LISTENING

Resharing or commenting have agency and likely clear intentionality, but consider other ways of "reacting" to a post online (👍❤️😮 😡😢⚠️😀). The real world communicative implications of engagement with a meme are difficult to parse in text form, but let's give it a try. Here's how it works in practice — In many cases, the social media system/algorithm notices any reaction at all (liking, sad face, angry face, heart). Consequently, that reaction will register on one's own feed and in the feed of one's followers. So if Jill were to react to a piece of media (meme or otherwise) on her page — even if that reaction was dismissive or accidental or simply polite and non confrontational (the very thing someone might do in a face to face conversation) Jill's interaction would propel that post to the top of feeds sorted by recency and would also publicize Jill's reaction to those whom Jill is connected with and beyond. An attempted innocuous simple smiley face emoji reaction might reverberate well beyond its intentionality.

LISTENING

Thus far, most of our focus has been message creation and sharing. Communication, after all, is an audience-centered phenomenon. Communication involves the sending and receiving of messages. Often overlooked (or taken for granted) is the essential element of communication, listening, which encompasses everything from physically receiving, selecting, attending/organizing, interpreting, negotiating, responding — and then the audience moving through the same process, often overlapping in real-time.

Rather than attempt to break down the complex process by which an individual might receive and process a meme, let us instead consider the potential obstacles to successful meme/message reception. Common barriers to listening discussed in the communication literature include:

1. Incomprehensibility,

2. Message overload,

3. Message complexity,

4. Environmental distraction,

5. Preoccupation / personal thoughts or concerns,

6. Prejudgments (preconceptions, bias, prejudice),

7. Lack of effort,

8. Reacting to emotionally laden language (triggering), and

9. Not differentiating between listening styles.

Memes (with transactionality built in) naturally highlight the listening component of communication— "the process of receiving and responding to others' messages" (Adler, 2021, p.). Consider the barriers that might shape the reception of any particular meme by any particular person or audience. One other helpful concept useful for our conversation, punctuation. The plot of a narrative has been described as "the logic that makes meaningful the events that precede the story's conclusion." Punctuation helps the listener follow the plot. "Before we can attribute meaning to communication, we must establish boundaries" (Wood, 2016, 69). Punctuation (not the marks) is the communication process by which we establish these boundaries. Knowing when a particular communication starts and ends or who started it can be extremely helpful when orienting oneself.

Another important part of online orienteering is coming to grips with time and how it works online, or the rhetorical term **chronemics**. Asynchronous communication occurs when there is a gap in time when a message is sent and received. Synchronous communication occurs in real time. Messages posted years ago might appear in your feed as if they were posted today, and a person, Ryan, might be reasonably let down if he sees his friend Troy is online, sends Troy a message, sees that his Troy has read the message, and then gets no response in return. Successful negotiation of the worlds of synchronous and asynchronous communication is a mark of communication competence.

COMMUNICATION MISCONCEPTIONS

Our focus on all of the things communication can do ultimately leaves us vulnerable to several misconceptions or inconvenient truths. Memes might actually help us see these misconceptions even more clearly. A commonly identified misconception, not all communication seeks understanding. It is a flawed assumption that the goal of all communication is to maximize understanding between communicators; instead, social rituals we enact every day attempt to influence others. Deliberate ambiguity and deception are examples of communication in which understanding is not the primary goal. Recent studies have found that false messages spread faster than truthful messages, and it's not difficult to find the role memes can play in this story.

More communication is not always better. In fact, it can often make things worse. Memes can exacerbate problems because they are so easily shared. Communication will not solve all problems because even the best-timed and best-planned communication cannot fix all problems. A well-timed, well-intentioned, expertly crafted, clear-eyed meme can still result in problems when factoring in the audience and the asynchronous nature of receiving online posts. Memes are subject to the same potential pitfalls of any communication or art. These potential pitfalls are only magnified by the rate of transmission, ease of creation, and richness of content. Another misconception is that people tend to see good or effective communication as a natural ability. Effective meme creation, like good communication, requires the coordinated use of skills. In decades past, these skills would have been bundled under multimedia or arts and crafts. But now, graphic design and narrative consistency can be the stuff of relationships, the stuff of advertising, and the stuff of everyday life. Communication, like breathing, is so commonplace that without concerted effort, it can go unnoticed.

WHY WE CONNECT WITH MEMES, ONE EXPLANATION

Let us consider a viable explanation for some of the power behind memetic communication. Memes carry with them an element of kitsch — something that, "No matter how we scorn it . . . is an integral part of the human condition (Kundera, 1984, 256). Oxford English Dictionary (2021) defines **kitsch** as "art, objects, or design considered to be in poor taste because of excessive garishness or sentimentality, but sometimes appreciated in an ironic or knowing way." This definition is a good start, but I'd like to push it a bit further. The relationship between memetic communication and kitsch can be seen in how the receiver relates to the content. This particular connection between kitsch and the seeing, making, and doing of rhetoric and communication, was first brought to this author's attention by the inimitable rhetoric scholar, Dr. Joshua Gunn (2008), in "For the Love of Rhetoric, with Continual Reference to Kenny and Dolly." Kitsch, not unlike mimetic communication, is often dismissed as unimportant or even trash — but the power that makes kitsch, kitsch is necessary to isolate what makes memes meme.[6]

> The feeling induced by kitsch must be a kind the multitudes can share. . . . Kitsch causes two tears to flow in quick succession. The first tear says: How nice to see children running on the grass! The second tear says: How nice to be moved, together with all mankind, by children running on the grass! It is the second tear that makes kitsch kitsch. The brotherhood of man on earth will be possible only on a base of kitsch. (Kundera, 2020, 251)

The power of kitsch lies in the experience of connecting with an individual connecting to a thing in itself, and then connecting to society at large. Memes, however, also present the opportunity for a heretofore unacknowledged, third tear to flow — in which the message recipient relates to the particular person, the poster or sharer of information — how nice to be moved in a similar way to this particular person I know and love — my friend, my mother, my schoolmate and I share this now[7], how beautiful — something

---

[6]Though my basic understanding of, and confusion regarding kitsch and camp I owe to Susan Sontag, this particular connection to rhetoric was first brought to this author's attention by the inimitable rhetoric scholar, Dr. Joshua Gunn, in "For the Love of Rhetoric, with Continual Reference to Kenny and Dolly." As he sought to explore rhetoric's connection to love as both "stupidity" and also transcendent-soul-mate-level "identification", Gunn revealed that a core power of rhetoric was akin to the power responsible for the influence of kitsch. Like a Bach fugue of intellectual play, the depths of which are beyond the scope of this chapter, Gunn wraps together the kitsch of the Dolly Parton/Kenny Rogers pop song, Islands in the Stream with the Hemingway novel of the same name, and another from the same poetic sermon of John Donne — Intentionally or not, Gunn is clearly in conversation with Sontag — who in her attempt to distinguish kitsch from camp wrote of For Whom the Bell Tolls, the film version of the Hemingway novel (the other novel title that was derived from the John Donne poem), the scathing critique, that it was "bad to the point of being laughable, but not bad to the point of being enjoyable." I've included this example for multiple reasons: 1.) This level of depth and specificity — mashups with multi-layered references — might seem daunting in text form — consider then that it is actually quite common when it comes to memes, 2.) Memes are able to exist among and between the worlds of seriousness and kitsch and camp — they easily walk the line, and 3.) Because it is the mimetic form / the medium of meme-based communication that delivers this power (not the content)

[7]Recall from chapter 1, "Memes can really only exist as a hybrid between the underlying message within the memes and the audience that is there to observe the meme." This idea of shared responsibility bolsters this kitsch connection.

skin to rhetorical identification or even consubstantiation, terms related to how individuals realize their connectedness. Memes create opportunities for more and provide easier access to identification and consubstantiation[8].

30andTired
@30andTired

Gas pump: Please see cashier

Me: Absolutely not

Figure 16: An example of a memetic tweet that creates a sense of identification and consubstantiation among the community that retweets this post. (Source: https://twitter.com/30andTired/status/1372168721901490186?s=20)

When my partner comes across this meme shared by a friend, she connects with the content directly (the first tear), with the fact that she is in a larger community of individuals who experience this in their lives the second tear, connection, and validation, the opposite of marginalization). She also has an instant connection to the friend or relation who shared the message (the third tear). It's more than simply relatability, and it's more than knowing

---

[8]Identification and consubstantiation are terms used in rhetorical theory and criticism. Burke explains this concept with two entities, A and B. "A is not identical with his colleague, B. But insofar as their interests are joined, A is identified with B. Or he may identify himself with B even when their interests are not joined, if he assumes they are, or is persuaded to believe so... In being identified with B, A is 'substantially one' with a person other than himself. Yet at the same time, he remains unique, an individual locus of motives. Thus he is both joined and separate, at once a distinct substance and consubstantial with another." "Consubstantiality may be necessary for any way of life," Burke says. And thus rhetoric, as he sees it, potentially builds community. It can tear it down as well. In the end, rhetoric relies on an unconscious desire for acting-together, for taking a 'sub-stance' together"

you aren't alone. It's connection. Beyond this, one can like, react, respond, (re)share, or remix the post and make it her own. Memes always allow this next-level engagement. All of these tears fall and are often wiped away, quickly. Put simply, "It's funny, you have that heightened experience, and then you go back to scrolling" (Canta, 2017).

It's important to remember that communication is an audience-centered phenomenon, and one's interpretation is one's own until one shares it. Consider the tale of how the above image, a pretty straightforward example of a play on words (nobody gets ME like you do) mixed with an impact font comic image macro meme, came to this chapter. As it turns out, this image that I had come across, in a different form, on social media, originated as a greeting card — a shareable meme that was also intended to be shareable in the real world — a fitting example for this chapter. That this sentiment is on the front of a greeting card meant to be shared implies, however, that the recipient isn't alone — in fact (playing on the phrase nobody gets ME like you do), it's likely that the sender is in on the joke too. But when I looked into the origins of the image I found that it was produced by a company and housed on their website. It's name? *Kitsch Noir*. When I read the name of the website the second tear fell, and I knew I had found my example.

Figure 17: Kitsch Noir

"AND THEREFORE NEVER SEND TO KNOW FOR WHOM THE BELL TOLLS; IT TOLLS FOR THEE..."

During the 2020 presidential election, Michael Bloomberg's rise in media attention, and though short-lived, his concomitant rise in the polls, was accompanied by a flurry of stories choosing to focus on his enlistment of meme creators to support his campaign. The infamous Fyre Festival — a blatant attempt to sell hype — known for its flameout and memorialized by countless news exposes and at least two documentaries, served as a cultural and meme-able moment[9]. However, it was these very promoters and meme creators behind the Fyre Festival that Bloomberg enlisted for his campaign. The Bloomberg campaign came to an end soon thereafter, but that might have been predicted by famed art critic Clement Greenberg, who in 1939 argued: "machine-made kitsch can undersell the native handmade article."

OTHER RELATED THEORIES THAT SHAPED THIS CHAPTER AND SHOULD BE A PART OF DISCUSSIONS OF MEMES MOVING FORWARD

Speech Act theory - "A theory of language is a theory of action"- Greig E. Henderson and Christopher Brown. Communicative acts imply agency on the part of the audience (Reich, 2011). Memes are communicative/speech acts. Memes can only exist in a world in which the audience participates. Speech act theory's central focus

---

[9]Criticism and ridicule, Detailed here: https://www.nytimes.com/2020/02/13/style/michael-bloomberg-memes-jerry-media.html, https://www.theverge.com/2020/2/13/21136160/bloomberg-2020-meme-instagram-influencers-campaign-marketing-fyre-festival-promoters, & https://people.com/politics/mike-bloomberg-campaign-is-paying-social-media-influencers-to-post-political-memes-online/

on agency can and should inform discussions of memetic communication.

Symbolic Interactionism - Embedded in communication's core principles is the theory that humans interact with their worlds through symbols and their understandings, interpretations, or relationships to those symbols. Language is symbolic, and communication is a negotiation between people with their own relationships to those symbols.

Uses and Gratifications theory - Focusing on the agency of the consumer of media and information, uses and gratifications theory operates from the perspective of an audience that seeks out and engages with material/media In an effort to satisfy their needs[10].

MEMES AND THE DARK SIDE OF COMMUNICATION

As is often the case, educators and proponents of communication education spend significantly more time focusing on the good — the ways in which communication and memes as communication can improve our lives and our relationships — than the bad, the shady, or the dark side of communication. For many years it was the part of the discipline less studied, less often acknowledged directly[11]. The dark side, however, is often more salient. Because effective

---

[10]These needs are distinct from the needs discussed elsewhere in this chapter — uses and gratifications needs fulfillment: cognitive needs (intellectual), affective needs (emotional), personal integrative needs (identity or self-focused), social integrative needs (relationship focused), and tension-free needs (no drama escapism).

[11]Spitzberg and Cupach (2011) tracked the prevalence of dark side topics in social science literature — This list, though not comprehensive, represented a view of the topics observed in dark side literature: anger, bad conversations, breaches of propriety, bullying, communicative apprehension, communicative incompetence, deception, depression, disaffinity, discouragements, fatal attractions, hurt feelings, internet deception, internet pathology, internet unwanted sexual attention, irritations by partner, jealousy, loneliness, marital divorce, marital "failure", negative emotions, pathological internet use, privacy seeking-aggressive, profanity, rejection, social inadequacy, sexual aggression, sexual harassment, shyness, social stress, stalking, swearing, teasing, threats, troublesome relationships, and violence.

meme creation can lead to highly successful self-contained nuggets of communication, the deleterious effects of memetic communication are also highly powerful/successful/salient/magnified. Though memes can provide outsiders access/easy entry to a particular topic, memes can also focus messages (in terms of intensity, density, richness) in support of dark side subjects/forces—potentially magnifying the effects of traditional forms of communication on the matter[12].

It is precisely because memes have become so commonplace that we must also consider the dark forces they so readily empower. Just as memes are sent and received to serve productive instrumental or relational goals, they are just as easily employed to serve[13] the dark side.

Violent and dangerous rhetoric can quickly gain steam via mimetic communication. Recall the three tears and the relationship between memes and kitsch. Those tears represent an individual connecting to the content, to the larger world, and to other specific individuals. Memes, due in part to this multipronged power of connection, can also, unfortunately, magnify connections for individuals experiencing negative or destructive thoughts and emotions. Individuals can find connection in, through, and to hateful or hurtful memes, and communities revolving around an identity of hurt or perceived victimization can gain strength through use of easily shareable/spreadable/remixable content like memes. The relatability of certain elements of a meme can make its initial reception more palatable, but the simple relatable message can smuggle a darker cache of messages. The incel community serves as a troubling case study of the work memes can do to expand the power of the dark side. As Cauterucci (2018) wrote in "Incel Memes Aren't a Joke: How Playful

---

[12]Examples include depression, anxiety, bullying, loneliness / isolation, violence/aggression, stalking, sexism, rape, sexual misconduct, matters of consent, misinformation, misogyny, and racism.

[13]The strongest pieces of evidence come from the use of misogyny from the Incel community (Dynel, 2020), the use of othering by the Pizzagate community (Lumsden, 2019) or even general groupthink behaviors

Propaganda Can Mask a Dangerous and Toxic Culture"

These insular communities have developed an in-group lingo that's tricky for outsiders to parse. When a community that's highly anonymous, decentralized, and often contradictory becomes fodder for memes, which are easily stripped of their provenance and edit history, it becomes extremely difficult for observers to understand and contextualize what they're seeing. Memes can provide crucial insight into what's really going on in incel forums. They can also warp the truth. Whether a meme is a bit of primary-source incel doctrine, a hyperbolic riff on an in-joke, or a work of satire can be impossible to determine if you don't spend hours a day steeping yourself in the native language of incel culture.

Incel culture's online insularity helped to create the conditions for documented real world spillover effects – In 2014, in Isla Vista (near UC Santa Barbara), six people were murdered and fourteen were injured by a single perpetrator. This was perhaps the first time the term incel made it into popular discourse. Incels received even more attention when in 2018 an incel-led vehicle ramming terrorist attack left ten people dead in Toronto. Incel memes and other content have flourished in the wake of these attacks. The connection(s) between dark side insularity and memes isn't only problematic when it leads to mass murder.

MEMES ARE ESSENTIAL TO UNDERSTANDING THE WORLD AS IT IS TODAY

It's sufficient to state that any attempt to understand communication must include an understanding of communication done on the internet in its effort to understand communication. And if we intend to do that, then we, as scholars, must grapple with memes. "The more we can understand memes and increase our overall meme literacy, the more we can understand the language people are speaking on the web" (Polgar, 2020).

But once again — *Meme Life* recognizes the expansion of the real world into internet land and vice versa. It's not just that understanding memes can help us understand the internet, it's that a better working knowledge of memes brings about a richer experience of life, more broadly, of life itself. A discussion of communication "as it exists online" necessitates an understanding of context. This book is being written in 2021 — literally every word of it was written in the context of pandemic communication and in the wake of the most significant influx/exponential arrival of users to the internets. Sure, the landscape of the internet is and always has been changing/growing, but communication, as it exists online today, is so much more closely aligned with the "real world" than it has ever been, working, playing, living, from home. Family dinners, birthday celebrations, conference calls, first dates, breakups, interviews, exploration of kinks, all of these things are happening in our kitchens, living rooms, and home offices. And memes are with us in all of this.

Communication courses and textbooks have long included messages like technology is most alienating when it's used as a substitute for human interaction (Adler, Rosenfeld, & Proctor, 2021). Scholars have long studied and debated how mediated communication affects relational quality. Mediated communication might, in some cases, have a negative impact on closeness, connection, and conversation quality. However, social media can also be rich and satisfying and can be used to improve one's connections. It can make the world a darker place, or it can make communication brighter. Scholars were asking these questions well before the Covid-19 pandemic forced changes in the way we live and communicate. The debates over the links between mediated communication and well-being weren't settled by the time the pandemic struck.

We didn't have the ability to opt-out of electronic communication if we wanted to stay in touch with our loved ones and the world beyond. Despite the many documented and potential drawbacks of online communication serving as the primary and, in many cases, sole option for communicating and maintaining personal and professional relationships, it has become the status quo, the oft-heard, new normal. Our communication technologies allowed us to keep some form of connection, and memes have done a lot of the work. It is going to be a struggle to catch up and make sense of how the world has changed and continues to change. It's going to take an awful lot of swimming to keep our heads above the water, but at least, unlike the fish, we know it's water. Despite our conversations here, memes will continue to present both challenges and opportunities for the foreseeable future, but,

> Because of today's terrific speed-up of information moving, we have a chance to apprehend, predict and influence the environmental forces shaping us – and thus win back control of our own destinies (McLuhan, 1969).

Using the same quote at the end of the chapter that you used at the beginning.

Works Cited

Adler, R. B., Rosenfeld, L. B., & Proctor, R. F. (2021). *Interplay: The process of interpersonal communication (15th Ed.)*. Oxford.

Canta, A. (2017). *Diamond Jesus: Beauty, kitsch, and the world of Memes*. Retrieved June 6, 2021 from: https://www.youtube.com/watch?v=rXNhNp5qgno

de Saint Laurent, C., Glaveanu, V., & Chaudet, C. (2020). Malevolent Creativity and Social Media: Creating anti-immigration communities on Twitter. *Creativity Research Journal, 32*(1), 66-80.

Dresser, S. (2019). *Can You Step in the Same River Twice? Wittgenstein v Heraclitus*. Retrieved June 7, 2021 from: https://aeon.co/ideas/can-you-step-in-the-same-river-twice-wittgenstein-v-heraclitus

Dynel, M. (2020). Vigilante Disparaging Humour at r/IncelTears: Humour as Critique of Incel Ideology. *Language & Communication, 74*, 1-14.

Eberly, R. (2007). *Seeing, Making, and Doing: Rhetoric, Public Scholarship, and the Voices of Democracy*. University of Wisconsin-Madison.

Golder, A. (2018). *17 Memes that'll only make sense to people who look at a lot of memes*. Retrieved June 7, 2021 from: https://www.buzzfeed.com/andyneuenschwander/17-memes-that-youll-need-prior-meme-knowledge-to-u

Goldman, A., and Vogt, P.J. (2016). *#83 Voyage into Pizzagate*. Retrieved June 7, 2021 from: https://gimletmedia.com/shows/reply-all/emhwl5

Jansson-Boyd, C. (2010). *Consumer Psychology*. McGraw-Hill.

Kundera, M. (2020). *The Unbearable Lightness of Being*. Faber & Faber.

Lumsden, K. (2019). '"I Want to Kill You in Front of Your Children" Is Not a Threat. It's an Expression of a Desire': Discourses of online abuse, trolling and violence on r/MensRights. In K. Lumsden & E. Harmer (Eds.), *Online Othering* (p. 91-115). Palgrave Macmillan.

Lunsford, A. A., Wilson, K. H., & Eberly, R. A. (2009). *The SAGE Handbook of Rhetorical Studies*. SAGE.

McGgonigle, K. (2013). How to Make Stress Your Friend. Retrieved June 7, 2021 from:Presented at Ted Global 2013 https://www.ted.com/talks/kelly_mcgonigal_how_to_make_stress_your_friend?language=en

Norden, E. (1969). *Marshall McLuhan: A candid conversation with the high priest of popcult and metaphysician of media*. Retrieved June 7, 2021 from: https://www.nextnature.net/story/2009/the-playboy-interview-marshall-mcluhan

Nissenbaum, A., & Shifman, L. (2020). Laughing Alone, Together: Local user-generated satirical responses to a global event. *Information, Communication & Society*, 1-18. doi: 10.1080/1369118X.2020.1804979

O'Sullivan, P. B. & Carr, C. T. (2017). Masspersonal Communication: A model bridging the mass-interpersonal divide. New Media & Society. 20(3), 1161-1180. Advance online publication. 1461444816686104. doi:10.1177/1461444816686104

Polgar, D. R. (2020). *Why Understanding Memes Is Important To Grasping What People Are Really Saying In 2020*. .Retrieved June 7, 2021 from: https://www.forbes.com/sites/davidryanpolgar/2020/06/04/why-understanding-memes-and-internet-humor-is-important-to-grasping-what-people-are-really-saying-in-2020/?sh=38910d914da2

Spitzberg, B. H., & Cupach, W. R. (2007). *The Dark Side of Interpersonal Communication*. Lawrence Erlbaum Associates.

Sontag, S. (2018) Notes on *"Camp."* Penguin Random House.

Varey, R. (1999). Marketing, Media, and McLuhan: Rereading the prophet at century's end. *Journal of Marketing, 63*(3), 148-153. doi:10.2307/1251781

Verderber, K. S., & MacGeorge, E. L. (2015). Inter-Act: *Interpersonal communication: Concepts, skills, and contexts (14th Ed.)*. Oxford University Press.

Williams, K. D., & Zadro, L. (2001). Ostracism: On being ignored, excluded, and rejected. In M. R. Leary (Ed.), *Interpersonal Rejection* (p. 21–53). Oxford University Press.

Wood, J.T. (2016). *Communication Mosaics: An introduction to the field of communication (8th Ed)*. Cengage.

Zidani, S. (2018). Represented Dreams: Subversive expressions in Chinese social media as Alternative Symbolic Infrastructures. *Social Media + Society 4*(4) 1-10. doi: 10.1177/2056305118809512

CHAPTER AUTHOR'S BIO

Thomas Weston Adams III has been teaching college-level communication since the fall of 2005. Educated at Pepperdine, San Diego State, and Penn State universities, Tommy's academic interests are too numerous to list. He is perhaps most interested in relationships and rhetoric with a focus on communication technology, democracy, and deliberating across differences. For the past several years he has been pivoting to a more relationship-focused understanding of communication. Devoted to helping improve the lives of his fellow Kentuckians, Tommy teaches at Bluegrass Community & Technical College and serves as a member of Wolfe County Search and Rescue. Tommy lives in Winchester with his partner and his dog(s) where he works to give connection and adventure and play the serious pursuit they deserve. Tommy has been running every single day since October 2018 and doesn't intend to break his streak anytime soon.

CHAPTER 8: MEMES AS A PERFORMANCE ACT

ELIZABETH COZAD-HOWARD
& JERMAINE MCGHEE

Communication has often been measured as a broad term that illustrates and explores different ways to express and disseminate information. Within a societal context, memes, performance, and semiotics propose a vital means to communicate and offer distinction of cultural influence in a digital age. This chapter is charged with the intention of illuminating the interconnected environments of social digital platforms, memes, performance, culture, and semiotics from the phenomenological perspectives of a moving black body and a somatically aware mind.

Contemporary society has utilized digital platforms to market, commodify, enhance and engage with themselves and others. One might even offer that within varied digital platforms, such as Facebook, Twitter, Instagram, TikTok, and Snapchat, memes are a reliable way to transfer ideas, emotions, political affiliations, or even artistic prejudices and expressions. It is with that in mind, the idea of perpetuating memes as performance in a global society becomes a keystone option to communicate an extended bandwidth of concepts. The bedrock of communication and exchange of information is found here.

Author Jakub Nowak (2016) in Internet Meme as Meaningful Discourse focuses on memes as a type of consumed media identified as a cultural object distributed on the internet. Today's collective experience is given direct access to new media tools, reconstruction, and redistribution of popular culture content across various social platforms. Nowak feels this is the essence of popular culture through which cultural and political identities can be communicated and negotiated. Sharing can be performed for fun or to persuade, inform, or create discussion amongst users. The internet meme has become a significant modality for social, political, cultural, and consumer commodities (78). Multi-participant authorship across social media platforms conveys the performativity of popular culture; "Memes are like a lens focusing and magnifying a wide array of cultural phenomena of online popular culture(s)" (82).

We have been performing since before birth. Reaching, kicking, squatting, talking, pulling, walking... movement can become my performance, and no two performances are the same. Performance has become our involvement, our voice, our stories. According to history, performance reflects the action or process of carrying out or accomplishing an action, task, or function. As this keynote suggests, performance offers meaning and constitutes purpose in a societal-multimedia context. Scholar and author Amanda Cole states "performance cannot be taught, is learned unconsciously, is an innate skill" (pg. 46). This notion asserts the idea that performance is indicative of a deep and meaningful knowing within the self. Whether that performance was the act of witnessing the happening or participating in the activity. At some point, we all have performed and completed a performance.

Humans are constantly performing. The mundane action of walking, to the observer, can appear simple. Yet our walk is performance, an individual cadence, a natural rhythm. The way our foot strikes and connects is our way of advancing through space; that is performance. Marvin Carlson (2017) in *Performance: A Critical Introduction* defines the following:

the term "performance" has become extremely popular in recent years in a wide range of activities in the arts, in literature, and in the social sciences. As its popularity and usage has grown, so has a complex body of writing about performance, attempting to analyze and understand just what sort of human activity it is. [. . .] The recognition that our lives are structured according to repeated and socially sanctioned modes of behavior raises the possibility that all human activity could potentially be considered as "performance," or at least all activity carried out with a consciousness of itself. [. . .] If we consider performance as an essentially contested concept, this will help us to understand the futility of seeking some overarching semantic field to cover such seemingly disparate usages as the performance of an actor, of a schoolchild, of an automobile (Carlson, 2017, 25).

So it is essential to be able to observe performance and not appraise it as good or bad, but rather acknowledge it for being uniquely its own. Our question inside the question then becomes, what is not a performance, and must a performance be qualified as such by the observer, performer, or both? In the text *What is Performance*, author Richard Schechner (2013) clarifies for the reader the difference between 'is' and 'as' performance. He offers the following,

Certain events are performances and other events less so. There are limits to what "is" performance. But just about anything can be studied "as" performance. Something "is" a performance when historical and social context, convention, usage, and tradition say it is. Rituals, play and games, and the roles of everyday life are performances because convention, context, usage, and tradition say so. One cannot determine what "is" a performance without referring to specific cultural circumstances. There is nothing inherent in an action in itself that makes it a performance or disqualifies it from being a performance. From the vantage of the kind of performance theory I am propounding, every action is a performance. But from the vantage of cultural practice, some actions will be deemed performances and others not; and this will vary from culture to culture, historical period to historical period (Schechner, 2013, 30).

PERFORMING IN A SOCIAL MEDIA SPACE

As social media becomes a more integrated aspect of society in a viable social, cultural, and digital context, sharing experiences, gathering influence, notating moments, and depicting current events (in real time), memes emerge as a significant conception affirming communicative value.

In other words, a meme is a content and a structure that replicates by passing on via communication (one to one, one to many, or many to many). It requires a medium (channel) and an agent to be transmitted. Its framework of time is varied as it can be spread vertically and horizontally, and its reach depends on its duration, structure as well as the channel used to be transmitted. Its mobility, storage, and speed depend on the technologies available at a particular time (current computer technologies are as fast as viral). Its success in replication and mutability or adaptability depends on the social context where the meme is put into play, so it can remain in that context or be ignored. If it stays, it can be adapted by other social contexts (Castaño-Diaz, 2013).

The broad use of memes implicates the essential and confirmative nature of performance in a fresh way. The vast majority of internet users have seen and or utilized a meme in one way or another. For instance, memes can be used as humor, a response to questions, critical analysis, or non-verbal performative speech. The creation of memes includes intention and context and can differ from culture to culture (Grundlingh, 2018).

MEMES AND PERFORMATIVITY

Intention and context can be described through the action of performativity. Performativity is the power of language to affect change in the world: language does not simply describe the world but may instead (or also) function as a form of social action. The concept of performative language was first described by the philosopher John L. Austin who posited that there was a difference between constative language, which describes the world and can be evaluated as true or false, and performative language, which does something in the world. The relationship between performativity and memes may be further developed by the study of semiotics. One of the broadest definitions of semiotics is that of Umberto Eco, who states that "semiotics is concerned with everything that can be taken as a sign. Semiotics involves the study not only of what we refer to as ‹signs› in everyday speech, but of anything which ‹stands for› something else. In a semiotic sense, signs take the form of words, images, sounds, gestures and objects" (Chandler, 2017). Memetic communication takes on these signs as the signifier of communication to and within society. In looking further at memes as communal performance, we can then ask, how do memes communicate to society and how is that performance?

A widely used impression of performance is the action or process of carrying out or accomplishing an action, task, or function.

When applying this description to the concept of memes, which is an element of culture or system of behavior that may be considered to be passed from one individual to another, an alignment can be gathered by the closely knit terms. Furthermore, one could deem the usage of memes as a performance in itself. Yet the question of performance, memes, and the black body converging restricts the expansive capacity that the three terms imply.

When witnessing a meme posted on a digital social platform such as Instagram, the witness may encounter different emotional and physical responses. If the meme instigates a funny tone some will laugh; if the meme indicates dark humor or sarcasm, some will ponder its intent or even get upset. But when a meme highlights a black body, it articulates African Aesthetics. Bay Area-based choreographer and Associate Professor at City College of San Francisco, Launa (2016), defines African Aesthetics as "a paradigm, a set of suppositions, principles, and ideologies upon which the African American worldview is structured. It is a consciousness and responsiveness that emerged from the distinct style and values of the people of the African Diaspora living in America for hundreds of years."

Your grandma looking down from Heaven watching you cook chicken in an air fryer:

Figure 18: A representation of the African Aesthetic meme format, with an emphasis on cultural and media signs within the meme. Source: https://www.instagram.com/p/COmE7fXrNag/

Memes that emanate from black bodies offer an additional con-notation of communication. Black aesthetics are often simulated in popular culture, whether in hairstyle expression, fashion, social dances, or cultural nuance. One thing is certain: when one identifies the cool of any socio-popular happening, they identify the African Aesthetic (aesthetic of cool), which exhibits, "personal and artistic style, the eminence of royalty, stillness, composure and down to earth elegance with a touch of flamboyant and audacity." (14)

SEMIOTICS OF BLACK EXPRESSION WITHIN MEMES

Digital culture in a chosen "communal body" or shared space via social media allows the meme to represent both a performance and a unit of signification or use of semiotics. According to analyst Abdul Kariko (2013), semiotics is applied as a method to approach texts on media with an assumption that the media themselves are communicated through the elements of signs that they already carried. The signs that are carried on the media are also filled with certain interests that show their own complexity because signs on media certainly never carry a single meaning. The semiotic tradition consists of a set of theories on how signs represent ideas, situations, feelings, materials, and conditions beyond the signs themselves. An analysis is conducted in particular on how the relationship between images and text, and how meanings connect with each other to form social messages, political messages, universal emotions, or even just humor and entertainment value.

Using the semiotic approach, research provides us with a method of focusing itself on signs and texts as study, and the ability to perceive and decipher the text and signs themselves. Images, gestures, tones, voices, music, objects, setting, or the combination of all of these, form a load of both conventional and contemporary entertainment and are part of the system of signs and semiotics.

Semiotics and memes both can be understood as a passing of social performance that allows the audience to transact and translate the meaning through their own social and cultural identity. Personal perception then becomes part of the transmission process and the connector of both memes and signs. Author Sara Cannizzaro quotes Deacon in her research on internet memes as internet signs: "A meme is a sign: some physical thing which, by virtue of some distinctive feature, can be recruited by an interpretive process within a larger system as re-presenting something else, conveying information into that system and reorganizing it with respect to that something else." (Cannizzaro, 2016).

Memes have the ability to communicate on a deep, meaningful level. Marco Ciorli (2017) states that the internet meme, "is a piece of culture". What greater signifier is necessary to implicate the interconnected nature of memes and semiotics through the investigations of imagery, text, and cultural evolution?

Transaction, translation, and transmission affect the communication or perception of the performative act of the meme itself through one's own social identity and cues. The variety and ability of a meme to be reconstructed brings to the forefront the collective process of meaning making (Cannizzaro, 2016). The performative act reaches beyond a simple means of communication and into the realm of embedded phenomenon through interactive social signs as signifying units. This "participatory culture" emerges to bring together these and other perspectives to further describe the social relevance of memes and their performative action in media communication. Through the perspective of cultural production, the synchronous communication of memes provides a shared experience of performance on both an emotional and cultural level (Ciorli, 2017).

REDEFINING PERFORMANCE VIA MEMES

Beyond the academic definition and the origin of memes is the use of communication through internet networks. This reproduction and transmission are important to identify as both performative and communicative, and as the results of action. Other concepts linked to the memes' properties uncovered in The Selfish Gene by Dawkins (1976) are the competition as well as its role in the development of the replicators. With this concept, the author points to the core of the Darwinian theory: the effect that environmental pressure exerts over replicators and how the competition for resources and space shapes them, as well as how more successful mutations can maintain, multiply, and compete with other memes in the same space.

From a performative standpoint, this brings us back to the lens of seeing and being seen through content creation and audience engagement in a virtual world. Using concepts from communication theories, a meme can take on characteristics that interact and conform to various categories of communication (Castaño Diaz, 2013). In One Does Not Simply Send Memes, author Marco Ciorli speaks to a level of performance as locutionary, illocutionary, and perlocutionary. A locutionary act is the basic level of "performance" of the word. When people talk about something, they produce sounds that respect the grammar of a language and that refer to a state of being. On a second level, we perform an illocutionary act by doing something that emits words: the intended action is performed totally or partially through the production of a specific locution, such as claims, questions, promises, or begging. Finally, a statement could have the effect, creating a perlocutionary act, to the extent that the speaker succeeds in actually making an intended consequence (e.g., one can persuade someone, but not simply by saying it). Alexander (2006). This divides the idea of communicative performance in an ideal typical way, distinguishing ritual performances and modern "ritual-like" strategies: the level of (re)fusion among the elements that form cultural performances determines their level of success.

Ciorli goes on to argue that it is possible to observe a similar phenomenon in the role of internet memes in mediated communication. While in the contexts perceived as more asynchronous, there is a production of meanings and cultural references through the communication and production of internet memes (humorous or not). In the synchronous communication, these cultural frames represent reference for new proximity in contextual encounters. Clearly, the two dimensions are in dialogic relationship, because communication and memetic production themselves are permitted, as we have seen, by the sharing of meanings and practices.

Internet memes touch on performance meaning through a unique language and distinctive signs. They develop codification, meaning, distinction and inclusion in a social community through experience and memetic production. Collective social identities reach beyond mere entertainment and performance in the role the internet meme plays in production of those identities (Ciorli, 2017).

Creating and investigating to curate performative content builds our connection to community and offers insight into sociological environments that already exist (memes). Recognizing our experiences are not the same, our perceptions of the material will be unique and manipulated for individual indulgence through online encounters. Performative content provides a ritual of reaction, function and connection, a shared experience. The creator, observer, and media influencer are all layered with personal identities and connections through the ritual of performance and the perceived encounter. When content is created and shared, we bring our lived experiences, emotions, our daily lives into the ritual of performance.

In referencing the ritual of performance, we can take a closer look at audience reaction while observing or interacting with a performance. What do we want to provide our spectators? Whether the story inspired the meme or the meme found its way into the story, the collision becomes the collaborator, a melting or joining of the creator's mind and their performance. Choosing to participate in memetic performance, an audience member knows that they are going to receive, partake in, or bear witness to participatory action. They may be spectating for the first time or already be an avid follower who feels at home in this virtual space. How they receive the performance will be unique, arriving with their own social stories, beliefs, and personal experiences. The social media platform of choice is their "communal body," a space where the performance lives and is shared.

American history suggests culture can be defined as the customs, arts, social institutions, and achievements of a particular nation, people, or other social group. In a performative framework, culture is informed by the normative happenings induced by all those who perform or observe performances. The idea that preparation, reflection, and nuance capture the essence of the culture of performance isn't an unreasonable idea. Yet the black body in performance asserts a vital cultural implication often used in society and widely disregarded and devalued. The black body offers a point of reference to cultural norms indicative of the African Diaspora and African Aesthetics. The Chair of Intercollegiate Department of Africana Studies, Professor Sheila Walker (2015), states the African Diaspora explains "the contributions of the African continent and of people of African descent to the development, diversity, and richness of world civilizations and cultures, which constitute the common heritage of humankind" (494). Consequently, performances that utilize the black body perpetrate distinct notions of culture within performance that assert deeper meaning and visual subtlety.

The deductions gained by performance, memes, and semiotics represent a piece of the human experience. As the framework of communication develops the investigation of the term's performance, memes and semiotics demonstrate the widespread sharing and curation of web-based social and cultural content. The thought of using memes as an act of performance illustrates the action itself, validating a performative happening. Memes establish the embodied connection shared by many and has the capacity to affect change, function as language, and express purpose in digital settings. The shared social and cultural knowingness infuses one's phenomenological experience and is a direct result of personal involvement, tone, and intent, revealing the interconnected conditions of social media and digital platforms.

Works Cited

Alexander, J. C. (2006). Social Performance between Ritual and Strategy. In J.C. Alexander, B. Giesen, & J. L. Mast (Eds.), *Social Performance. Symbolic Action, Cultural Pragmatics, and Ritual* (pg. 29-90). Cambridge University Press.

Cannizzaro, S. (2016). Internet Memes as Internet Signs: A semiotic view of digital culture. *Sign Systems Studies*, 44(4). doi:10.12697/SSS.2016.44.4.05

Carlson, M. (2017). *Performance: A critical introduction*. Routledge.

Castaño Diaz, C.M. (2013). Defining and Characterizing the Concept of Internet Meme. *Revista CES Psicología*, 6(2),82-104.

Chandler, D. (2017). *Semiotics for Beginners*. Retrieved May 10, 2020, from http://www.visual-memory.co.uk/daniel/Documents/S4B/

Ciorli, M. (2017). *One Does Not Simply Send Memes: Performativity of Internet memes in synchronous mediated communication*. Retrieved May 10, 2021 from: https://www.researchgate.net/publication/317903441_One_Does_Not_Simply_Send_Memes_-_Performativity_of_Internet_Memes_in_Synchronous_Mediated_Communication.

Cole, A. (2019). What Is Performance? And Why Should We Teach It?. *Australian Journal of Music Education*, 52(2), 46-57

Dawkins, R. (2016). *The Selfish Gene (40th Anniversary Edition)*. Oxford University Press.

Grundlingh, L. (2018). Memes as Speech Acts. *Social Semiotics, 28*(2), 147-168. doi: 10.1080/10350330.2017.1303020

Kariko, A. (2013). *Analysis on Internet Memes using Semiotics*. Retrieved May 10, 2021 from: https://english.binus.ac.id/2013/06/24/analysis-on-internet-memes-using-semiotics/

Luana. (2016). *What Makes that Black? The African American Aesthetic in American expressive culture*. 1st ed., Lulu Press.

Nowak, J. (2016). Internet Memes as Meaningful Discourse: Toward a theory of multiparticipant popular online content. *Central European Journal of Communication,* *16*(5) doi: 10.19195/1899-5101.9.1

Schechner, R. (2013). *Performance Studies : An introduction* (3rd ed.). Routledge.

Walker, S. S. (2015). Milestones and Arrows: A Cultural Anthropologist Discovers the Global African Diaspora. *Journal of African American History, 100*(3), 494-521.

Ward, S.A. (2013). African Dance Aesthetics in a K–12 Dance Setting: From history to social justice. *The Journal of Physical Education, Recreation & Dance, 84*(7) 31–34. doi:10.1080/07303084.2013.817924.

CHAPTER AUTHORS' BIOS

Elizabeth Cozad-Howard is an Assistant Professor and the Director of Dance at Ohio Northern University where she instructs Ballet and Modern dance. She holds an MFA in dance from Saint Mary's College of California and a BFA in Dance from Wright State University. Cozad-Howard is a creative artist whose research is invested in the connection between self, performer, and audience through the use of creative expression, both physical and emotional; Her work is used to open conversations through art making and bringing awareness to the use of expressive movement as a means to physical, mental and emotional well being.

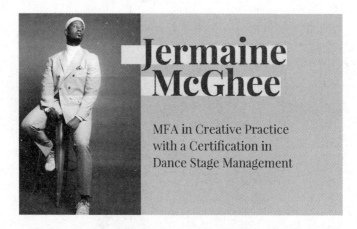

Jermaine McGhee

MFA in Creative Practice
with a Certification in
Dance Stage Management

Jermaine McGhee embodies a versatile and charismatic educator, dance artist, and choreographer. McGhee began training through the Education and Arts Enrichment program at North Carolina Dance Theatre, now Charlotte Ballet. In 2018 McGhee earned the BA in Performing Arts, May 2020 McGhee graduate with the MFA in Dance: Creative Practice, both from Saint Mary's College of California. McGhee's thesis research surrounding the exploration of African Aesthetics in American Culture supports his ongoing creative scholarship in black dance forms, and implementation of digital/social media platforms in shaping popular dance from the perspective of the black dancing body.

CHAPTER 9: MEMES AS A SOCIOLOGICAL ACT

Humans tend to gravitate towards others based on a series of essential demographic characteristics (being born in the same city, being in the same age bracket, having similar education levels, coming from related economic backgrounds, going to the same church, etc.), sharing the same psychographic motivations (having parallel value systems, holding common overarching beliefs, expressing identical attitudes about defined social elements, or performing corresponding behaviors towards others), or other markers that help us feel like we are together as a communal spirit (as opposed to being physically close together). Studying why people come together and how they interact is part of the field of sociology.

Specifically, we can examine a small sliver of the sociological field through the framework of understanding how group identities are formed through the interactions between group members and in-between groups. The nature of such interactions is based on how many members make up the group, the level of formality between members, and the locations in which those exchanges take place. In the past, sociological studies focused on a specific physical site that acted as the arena of those exchanges. However, it is fair to argue that sociology has escaped the need for a singular real-world place due to modern online interactions (Zhang & Dholakia, 2018).

Meme scholars using a sociological frame look for the patterns of interactions to conclude something about the groups they are studying. Those patterns arise when group members react collectively to social forces and cultural movements and happen most of the time because of one or more internal guiding principles that define the group interactions, such as:

1. customs which represent the past practices of the group

2. rituals that group members perform based on social factors, timing, and other cultural traditions

3. laws that maintain the social norms of the group

4. common moral beliefs and values that drive group members' behaviors and

5. other cultural rules that make up the daily routines of group members' lives

These guiding principles allow sociologists and meme scholars to define the group's scene, which is how group members see their ability to act within the group and how they coordinate with one another to accomplish anything as a collective (Grey, 2017).

This chapter will focus on the aspects of memetic culture that lend themselves to sociological study. Social psychology will be the binding force for this section of the book, as this chapter is designed to help therapeutic professionals work with clients to either create memes or discuss the use of memes in social interactions, as they relate those internal guiding principles that define group interactions. Memes express group customs by connecting aspects of popular culture to the past practices of the group. Rituals can be the performative elements of memetic artifacts. The other cultural rules can be part of the memetic layers described earlier. These elements are worth examining because the memes can help make the invisible aspects of society and culture visible. We will begin by addressing two of the common sociological markers one would use to explain social patterns.

MEMES AS DEMOGRAPHIC MARKERS

Sociological studies use demographic characteristics to establish how those social patterns relate to various populations. **Demographic characteristics** allow those studying a population to delineate separate groups within that more extensive population base to develop theories about how individuals react to different stimuli based on how other people who shared those demographic traits would respond. For example, we can look at how often white suburban Midwesterns under the age of eighteen go to a fast-food restaurant. White, suburban, Midwestern, and age are all demographic characteristics. Understanding common reactions based on shared demographic characteristics allows sociologists to craft paradigms that form theories regarding a society that other researchers can test and create experiments to generalize a given community and its members.

Memes tend to reflect demographic characteristics in the various layers. These reflections are **demographic markers**, as there are layers within the meme that are meaningful to a given subgroup of a population that share demographic characteristics (Liefbroer & Toulemon, 2010). A classic example of a demographic marker is near and dear to anybody that lives in Ohio. It is common to see a picture of a construction barrel being shared on social media with the words "The State Flower of Ohio." Construction barrels are a common occurrence in Ohio (as in other states) and have become part of the shared social experience of living in Ohio. Another shared social experience is the speed at which weather changes. All of these everyday occurrences are part of the daily lived happenings of an Ohioan.

Figure 19: Two examples of symbolic demographic markers within a meme. "Construction Barrel" memes are popular with those living in Ohio based on observational datasets and the weather memes speak to the living experiences of those in Ohio. Photo Sources: "Construction Barrel Monster" by ericmerrill is licensed with CC BY 2.0 from https://search.creativecommons.org/photos/7563a055-7976-411b-bdd8-d6340d58ef03; "50 Degrees" by "Mistakes on the Lake" from https://www.facebook.com/mistakesonthelake/posts/3527945770668111

Meme creators use those demographic markers to highlight how those subgroups differ from the general population. Those demographic markers are meaningful to the specific subset the meme is referencing. We discussed one type of demographic marker in the form of a meaningful symbol. These significant visual representations of a demographic group are the most recognizable and most often used. Referencing well-known people or locations within a meme can also act as a demographic marker. For example, the name Tim Misny will likely mean nothing to those living outside the Cleveland area or Northern Ohio. However, "Misny Makes Them Pay" (the slogan that Misny uses in advertisements) billboards are part of the outdoor landscape in that part of the country. Misny and his billboard are part of the memetic language for those that live in the region.

Figure 20: Another example of a demographic marker within a meme. "Misny Makes Them Pay" is a billboard that would have significance to those living in Northern Ohio. Source: "Mistakes on the Lake" Facebook page. https://www.facebook.com/mistake-sonthelake/posts/3518190781643610

Demographic markers functionally work the same as the popular culture content one would find within a meme. They require a person to have the cultural capital to understand the significance of those symbols, people, or locations. Unlike the popular culture content, a person's lived experiences traditionally provide enough cultural capital to surmise what the demographic markers mean. These modes of identifying others who share demographic characteristics make it easier to communicate and interact with others online by using aspects of their shared demographic experience as part of those online interactions. A person who used to tell stories about a group's hometown when interacting face-to-face can now use memes with significant images from back home when connecting with others online.

Demographic markers functionally work the same as the popular culture content one would find within a meme. They require a person to have the cultural capital to understand the significance of those symbols, people, or locations. Unlike the popular culture content, a person's lived experiences traditionally provide enough cultural capital to surmise what the demographic markers mean. These modes of identifying others who share demographic characteristics make it easier to communicate and interact with others online by using aspects of their shared demographic experience as part of those online interactions. A person who used to tell stories about a group's hometown when interacting face-to-face can now use memes with significant images from back home when connecting with others online.

It is fair to argue that demographic characteristics are a surface-level mode of sociological analysis. Those characteristics and markers partially come from the socioeconomic status of community members, which represents a wide variety of various aspects of daily life (from the health of the community to the lifestyle that they enjoy) and reflected in the multiple forms of communication that community members use (Wani, 2019). Other demographic components are surface-level observations of the community. The next level of sociological analysis as it relates to memes comes from a more profound place.

MEMES AS PSYCHOGRAPHIC MARKERS

Memes also show a community's collective beliefs, values, behaviors, and attitudes as expressed through artistic works. Unlike the demographic ones mentioned earlier, **psychographic characteristics** embody internalized aspects of the personality that manifest themselves into the individual's needs, wants, and desires (Leyva, 2017). **Psychographic markers** are the community's concrete representations of their needs, wants, and desires in the form of layers within a meme. Often psychographic markers are proxies for those needs, wants, and desires as those are too abstract to accurately show (for example, dollar bills representing wealth).

Memes are best at expressing the community's collective interests, specifically what community members spend their free time doing. The rationale for this ability is that most interests have recognizable symbols and signs that people would connect with a given hobby, passion, pastime, or fandom. It is not unusual for a community's collective interest to crossover in some of their demographic markers or characteristics. For example, long-distance runners in New York City would have merchandise for the Big Apple Marathon, or college students would express their political interest by joining Young America's Foundation, College Democrats, Young Ecosocialists, or Students for a Libertarian Society. All groups and events have symbols that tie demographic and psychographic characteristics into a base set of symbols that become those psychographic markers. Imagery of this nature is easy to incorporate into a meme and be recognized by others.

Another psychographic characteristic that memes can mark with signs is the lifestyles of community members. These markers are more than just the consumer behaviors they exhibit (even though that is a psychographic characteristic associated with lifestyle). **Lifestyle markers** express a collection of day-to-day activities that would resonate with most community members (Carducci, 2020). Motivations to perform those tasks are celebrated within memetic content and worth critically examining as part of the social life of a community member. Memes reveal this information even if community members themselves are not aware of the significance of their lifestyle.

The final psychographic characteristic to denote (beyond the beliefs, values, attitudes, behaviors, and opinions discussed earlier in this book) is how personalities are expressed within the community and (eventually) in the community's memes. The HEXACO Model of Personality Structure (Ashton et al., 2004) is a reasonable means to examine how aspects of personality are reflected in memes. Community members' honesty/humility, emotionality, extraversion, agreeableness, conscientiousness, and openness to experience become arguments within the meme about the general nature of the community. An example of how memes show **personality markers** would be when Canada is referenced in memetic content, reinforcing the stereotype of always apologizing and being too polite.

Psychographic markers are useful to examine in any memes as they represent internal aspects that community members shared. The popularity of those memes containing psychographic markers allows therapists and memetic researchers to focus on those markers and explain why members would highlight them in memes. This knowledge is vital, especially when the same psychographic marker appears over and over again. This thematic repetition happens when a psychographic quality embeds itself in the shared social experiences of the community.

MEMES AS SHARED SOCIAL EXPERIENCES

These connections between memes and the shared social experiences between community members depend on the type of community. There are six different types of these organizations that are worth denoting when addressing these shared social experiences, as those occurrences will vary depending on what maintains the cohesiveness of the community (Tilton, 2020). The memes from these communities will be fundamentally different as they are by-products of the community.

A **community of locus** (or location) typically has a similar set of "shared social experiences" reflected in geography, institutions, and social structures (like community organizations or government agencies) of a given region of the world that the community or audience has some permanence or semi-permanence to that given area. People in that community are tuned to the daily happenings of other community members through interactions associated with the various social institutions in the community (like churches, schools, or businesses). Your hometown is one such community of location. Online communities can be an extension of these types of communities. Both online and real-world interactions are based on members' familiarity with the daily happenings of those local institutions and social structures. Those interactions tell the story of the local community. Memes that reflect a community of locus tells those stories in memetic form.

Another type of community that develops shared social experiences would be those of **communities of convenience**, which are defined as communities that are temporarily together based on external factors that momentarily connect people. Community members form from an ad-hoc organization where none of the people are "bound" to the group for an extended period. Festivals and other short-term events (like Burning Man, South by

217

Southwest, or the Conservative Political Action Conference) tend to be the primary communities of convenience. It is important to note that people do not have to attend the event specifically to become members of that community. Those that are there will have stronger shared social experiences when compared to those that experience the event for a distance. Memes from these communities will revolve around icons (e.g., the SxSW logo), "inside jokes" about what happened there, or any other interaction that "you had to be there to experience."

Unlike communities of convenience, **communities of circumstance** are defined by community members' social status or life experiences rather than a given profession. Grad students tend to be a community of circumstance as they yet to become professionals in the field of study. It is not unusual for webcomics to be used as the central layer of memetic content shared by these communities (e.g., Ph.D. Comics) as they speak to those shared social experiences.

A group that is a more long-term version of this community would be a community of practice. **Communities of practice** share a common set of ethical standards, training, and skills to maintain the status quo and advance their occupation or vocation. Professionals who practice medicine would be one example of such a community. Members of the community bond over the labors it took to be a part of this group and often use jargon to define their profession within memetic content. Those struggles are part of the collective identity and are reflected in the memes created by community members.

One community is more internal in both the motivations and bonds than the previously listed communities. **Communities of purpose** are people going through the same process or trying to achieve a similar objective. Members of a community of purpose share common motivations, desires, and directions to meet their goals. Alcoholics Anonymous would seem to be an excellent example of this type of organization, as their focus is semi-permanent. Shared social experiences and memes from these communities are based on the stories that community members tell about going through the process or meeting their goals. The imagery and context related to these shared social experiences will be more concrete and meaningful than the previous communities' content, as it is purpose-driven.

Finally, a **community of interest** promotes the passions, knowledge base, and mutual respect of the criteria that define a hobby or pastime. For example, anime fans would be a community of interest. Community members use the hobby or pastime to guide interactions or communication with others, as it is the arena in which they are the most comfortable interacting with one another. These interactions or exchanges of information within the community will reinforce the shared knowledge base as layers within memetic content. Some anime titles and characters are more meaningful to the community of anime fans. This meaningfulness allows memetic content to focus on those aspects of the hobby to create niche mediated works (e.g., subbing an anime scene to reflect the results of a national election).

All of these communities have different shared social experiences that are meaningful. Still, some of those social experiences cross communities to become significant in different ways (e.g., the hells of grad school ["community of circumstance"] become the bonding experience to college professors ["communities of practice"]).

MEMES AS A FORM OF SOCIAL AGENCY

Graduate students, much like other socially marginalized populations, are denied access to various aspects of social life in their given community (in this case, the academic world). They are not considered faculty members, nor are they really considered traditional students (read as undergraduate students). They also have limited rights on campus (at the time of this writing, most do not have the right to unionize). A casual observer would argue that they have little social agency. **Social agency** is the ability of people or groups in society to influence the daily actions of others, change their status within the community, represent themselves without others interfering, or be recognized as a member of the community (Trauger, 2008).

One of the areas that memes grant social agency is their ability to perform political participation within the community. **Political participation** in memetic content focuses on the actions that would normally be considered civic engagement to get others in the community to care and act upon issues that affect their community and learn more about civic topics that can improve community members' lives (Hanley, 2010). Involvement in the political realm of any community forces members to reduce those issues and topics to fit the context of memetic content. That reduction can turn more significant issues into slogans (e.g., Get Brexit Done, No Justice No Peace, #MeToo) or visuals (e.g., umbrellas for the Hong Kong protests, red ribbons for HIV/AIDS awareness, the peace symbol) that gain significance through consistent use across a multitude of platforms which use them for the same purpose.

Another way that memes provide social agency is that memes are the end result of creators having technological affordances due to newer communication technologies being readily available to socially marginalized populations (both in the form of hardware like inexpensive smartphones that are powerful enough to craft mediated content and software like social media services). These technological affordances also include "the lack of gatekeepers, easy dissemination of information, lower barriers to access, and so on" (Burton, 2019, 4) that grant users of those technologies more direct access to members of their community that they might not be afforded to in the real world (Bennett, Freelon, & Wells, 2010).

One final way that memes represent social agency is how they allow creators and users to express cultural resistance regarding how topics and issues are presented online by members of their community by shaping the narrative within the memes that they create. **Cultural resistance** happens when a community uses meaningful symbols from the general public or a powerful section in society to change or disrupt how those populations interpret the meaning of those symbols (Duncombe, 2002). Resistance happens in memetic content when the community treats popular culture content as a commodity that they can engage with, cooperate to create new content from the older works, and use those more contemporary works to "jam up" the cultural and creative industries that mass produce works of popular culture.

A natural way to sum up memetic content's role in developing social agency is related to how memes address changes in society. Communities will use the tools of communication available to them to express their thoughts, opinions, and beliefs about the world around them. Online communication has become an extension of how members declare their overall concerns for their communities. Memes give community members limited control of how they present themselves to the general public. Workers in a particular office might use memes from *The Office* (for mostly positive situations) or *Office Space* (for mostly negative situations) to represent their daily working environment. Exerting this form of power becomes a coping mechanism that acknowledges the stress one experiences and says something about it.

MEMES AS A FORM OF SOCIAL CAPITAL

There are two ways to think about social capital, especially as it relates to memetic content. Pierre Bourdieu's (2021) *The Forms of Capital* is the foundation of how we have defined capital throughout this book. Sociologists who study the concept of social capital frame the term around class arguments related to how one gains power within society.

Economic capital is what we would generally think about when describing capital. It is the ownership of the materials that allow an individual or organization to gain money. But there is also **cultural capital**, which is the knowledge of the difference between high and low culture within a society based on a cultural work's objective nature (physical goods vs. digital content), the embodiment of social norms (defining ourselves in society), institutional recognition (certified as belonging to a specific aspect of society), technical merit (having the skills to pay the bills), emotional maturity (being empathetic or sympathetic to certain social situations), and understanding national and cultural traditions.

Therefore, Bourdieu argues that the final form of capital is social, representing having connections with others to have the power to change what is happening within a given community. This long-form analysis of capital is only the first way to think about social capital as it denotes power structures within the society (Siisiäinen, 2000). The second way to think about social capital is more about building social engagement between community members.

A group of sociologists led by Lindon J. Robison (2012) proposed a second way to think about social capital in their article *The Relative Importance of Selfishness and Social Capital Motives*. Robison et al. argued that people attempt to gain social capital based on four dynamics. The first way people gain social capital is to build a strong connection with others in a community, which validates that their actions within the community reflect that person's true self and meets the community's behavioral standards. Secondly, people are looking for other's approval. Social capital in the form of support from the community is a representation of that approval. The third point is that people want to feel like they belong in society in some role. Social capital can be built in the form of a purpose, position, or station within an organization. Finally, social capital is pathos-driven. We help out others in the community based on feeling a sympathetic connection with community members. We spend that social capital as it increases our validation within the community and maintains our sense of belonging to the group. Both Bourdieu and Robison et al. help us understand why memes are a form of social capital.

We have touched on why meme scholars and psychological professionals could apply Bourdieu's definition of social capital to memes. They can influence people's perceptions about the topics and issues facing a community. We used them as a mode of communication to address the points that we consider valid as part of a political discussion or cultural dialogue. The combination of the various layers that make up a meme from the rhetorical position that we hold and, in turn, have the power to influence others' thoughts on those subjects. Bourdieu's writing would seem to support the claim that memes represent social capital.

The points raised by *The Relative Importance of Selfishness and Social Capital Motives* would also seem to support the claim that memes are a form of social capital. The meme creator expresses themselves through memetic content, hoping that the community will make the meme popular, thus validating the meme creator's experiences. A meme becoming popular means that the meme creator would see their work and message approved by the community. If a meme creator has several of their memes widely used

MEME LIFE

by the community, they would rightly claim that they belong to the community, as they have addressed the community's thoughts in a form that members can easily share.

Understanding memes as social capital means that a therapist can examine how their client connects with the rest of the communities they belong to and discuss how they contribute to the overall health of that community. Suppose a person feels a strong sense of belonging to a particular community. In that case, it is fair to argue that some aspects of the community resonate with the client's beliefs, values, attitudes, behaviors, opinions, or identity. For example, the Minecraft Community are bound together for their love of Minecraft, which is a gaming platform/open-world digital environment/place for online engagement. More likely than not, members of the Minecraft community believe in a broad definition of the concept of a game. One of the values that tends to connect community members is being creative in Minecraft is an admirable trait. Aspects of identity are more aesthetic in nature, as the blocky graphic of the game tends to be distinctive. People who post pictures of the Minecraft creations online are easily identified as members of the community, thus others can connect and communicate with those that show-off their love of the game. The collective community composition of beliefs, values, attitudes, behaviors, opinions, and identity form the foundations of most social movements.

MEMES AS THE GUIDEPOSTS FOR SOCIAL MOVEMENTS

Memes often make the movements spotlighted by hashtags, trending topics, and other social media functions more understandable to the average person. The combination of a humorous tone, highlighting the irony of a situation, pointing out the absur-

224

dity of an action, and using symbols that people will recognize makes it easy for movement organizers to explain what drives their movement and engage with people who might want to get involved. Topics and issues that the members of the movement care about are often part of the central messaging of those memes.

One such example of how memetic communication guides engagement with social movements came in 2014 in Colorado. Conservative activists attempted to reform the Advanced Placement U.S. History standards set by the College Board. They got three reform candidates elected to the Jefferson County School Board to inject curricular changes to the teaching of American history. Students and community members protested those changes by creating a memetic template that was "an irresistible invitation to remix historic facts and undermine conservative efforts to dictate how lessons from history were taught" (Foust & Weathers, 2021, 135) and using the Twitter hashtag #JeffCoSchoolBoard-History as a banner and a way to organize memetic content under one central theme. Some of the examples of tweets that used this memetic template included:

- Bay of Pigs was a very cute event where pigs were let loose on a bay in Cuba to symbolize freedom for everyone

- In 1787, Jesus wrote the US Constitution

- British give poor Indians blankets to keep them warm, no smallpox intended

- President Pinochet, with the support of his American backers, ushered Chile into a new era of prosperity

Tweets using the #JeffCoSchoolBoardHistory hashtags were used by those that opposed the standard reform to illustrate the absurdity of the position held by the reform candidate and high-light the damage that such candidates would have a school system (that is lowing the quality of education through these new "poorer" educational standards). The social movement›s goal was to remove the three school board members and return a sense of normality to the school system. Supporters of the #JeffCoSchoolBoardHistory movement met their goals as the memetic content provided the community with an "argumentative kernel" amplified through social media exchanges and local community interactions (Deur-ringer, 2015).

Ryan Milner (2013) has referred to this amplification of social issues through memes as "pop polyvocality," since the messaging of the problems is merely one of many voices being expressed within the meme. Using popular culture content as a platform to discuss issues central to the causes supported by a given movement means that the aspects of that content (in the form of characters, sayings, symbols, locations, or other imagery that found in graphic novels, television shows, video games, feature films, musical works, or any other creative product) are adding to the political discourse about those issues. One such example came from the Occupy Wall Street (OWS) movement.

Milner notes the memetic content created by activists and "cul-turejammers" (i.e., AdBusters) helped make the protest more visible, even when there was little media coverage focusing on Zuccotti Park (the central area near Wall Street where most of the demonstrations were taking place) and various other protests against the "unchecked capitalism" that lead to the 2008 worldwide economic collapse. Spreading memes on Twitter, Reddit, Tumblr, and YouTube helped demonstrators connect with others that were supportive of the OWS movement. Those memes also introduced new concepts to the general public, like The People›s Microphone, participatory democracy, and the Assembly Hand Signals (Radovac, 2014).

It should not be surprising that memes are used this way by social movements. All successful social movements embed a centralizing message within a slogan, sign, or symbol that protestors and supporters can easily repeat to unify the group. Hashtags and memes are the digital components of this unifying communication. Slogans ring in the air, signs move with the people, symbols are left behind as marks of remembrance, and these digital works move in a digital environment to promote the ideas of these movements. Both hashtags and memes can promote the agendas of social movements because they can bridge the offline-online barrier and address the "digital dualism" problem (Jurgenson, 2011). These mediated works allow the general public to shift their focus from the memes associated with a given hashtag to the real-world impact of that hashtag›s social movement.

MEMES AS THE EXTENSION OF THE SOCIAL NETWORK

Memes often make the movements spotlighted by hashtags, trending topics, and other social media functions more understandable to the average person. The combination of a humorous tone, highlighting the irony of a situation, pointing out the absurdity of an action, and using symbols that people will recognize makes it easy for movement organizers to explain what drives their movement and engage with people who might want to get involved. Topics and issues that the members of the movement care about are often part of the central messaging of those memes.

One such example of how memetic communication guides engagement with social movements came in 2014 in Colorado. Conservative activists attempted to reform the Advanced Placement U.S. History standards set by the College Board. They got three reform candidates elected to the Jefferson County School Board to inject curricular changes to the teaching of American history. Students and community members protested those changes by creating a memetic template that was "an irresistible invitation to remix historic facts and undermine conservative efforts to dictate how lessons from history were taught" (Foust & Weathers, 2021, 135) and using the Twitter hashtag #JeffCoSchoolBoardHistory as a banner and a way to organize memetic content under one central theme. Some of the examples of tweets that used this memetic template included:

- Bay of Pigs was a very cute event where pigs were let loose on a bay in Cuba to symbolize freedom for everyone

- In 1787, Jesus wrote the US Constitution

- British give poor Indians blankets to keep them warm, no smallpox intended

- President Pinochet, with the support of his American backers, ushered Chile into a new era of prosperity

Tweets using the #JeffCoSchoolBoardHistory hashtags were used by those that opposed the standard reform to illustrate the absurdity of the position held by the reform candidate and highlight the damage that such candidates would have a school system (that is lowing the quality of education through these new "poorer" educational standards). The social movement›s goal was to remove the three school board members and return a sense of normality to the school system. Supporters of the #JeffCoSchoolBoardHistory movement met their goals as the memetic content provided the community with an "argumentative kernel" amplified through social media exchanges and local community interactions (Deurringer, 2015).

Ryan Milner (2013) has referred to this amplification of social issues through memes as "pop polyvocality," since the messaging of the problems is merely one of many voices being expressed within the meme. Using popular culture content as a platform to discuss issues central to the causes supported by a given movement means that the aspects of that content (in the form of characters, sayings, symbols, locations, or other imagery that found in graphic novels, television shows, video games, feature films, musical works, or any other creative product) are adding to the political discourse about those issues. One such example came from the Occupy Wall Street (OWS) movement.

Milner notes the memetic content created by activists and "culturejammers" (i.e., AdBusters) helped make the protest more visible, even when there was little media coverage focusing on Zuccotti Park (the central area near Wall Street where most of the demonstrations were taking place) and various other protests against the "unchecked capitalism" that lead to the 2008 world-wide economic collapse. Spreading memes on Twitter, Reddit, Tumblr, and YouTube helped demonstrators connect with others that were supportive of the OWS movement. Those memes also introduced new concepts to the general public, like The People›s Microphone, participatory democracy, and the Assembly Hand Signals (Radovac, 2014).

It should not be surprising that memes are used this way by social movements. All successful social movements embed a centralizing message within a slogan, sign, or symbol that protestors and supporters can easily repeat to unify the group. Hashtags and memes are the digital components of this unifying communication. Slogans ring in the air, signs move with the people, symbols are left behind as marks of remembrance, and these digital works move in a digital environment to promote the ideas of these movements. Both hashtags and memes can promote the agendas of social movements because they can bridge the offline-online barrier and address the "digital dualism" problem (Jurgenson, 2011). These mediated works allow the general public to shift their focus from the memes associated with a given hashtag to the real-world impact of that hashtag's social movement.

FERDINAND TÖNNIES AND MEMETIC COMMUNITIES

Therapeutic professionals and memetic scholars can cultivate an appreciation for memetic communities by understanding real-world communities and how they develop over time. A reasonable way to begin this process is by examining the work of one of the foundational scholars in this field. Ferdinand Tönnies refined the theoretical comprehension of community development at the end of the 19th century. His 1887 book Gemeinschaft und Gesellschaft (Community and Society) looked at the differences between the rural areas of Germany with their small and traditional villages and the modern urban cities with the industrial infrastructures.

The rural villages of Germany fit the **Gemeinschaft** model of community development as personal ties enhanced by in-person interactions define those social groups. Traditional communal rules allowed the community to develop an overall cooperative social organization based on a standard set of values and beliefs shared by most, if not all, community members. All members use personal interactions to organize the community's priorities that align with their beliefs and values. Community spirit and traditions were based on what the community feels emotionally attached to and their sense of moral obligation. Current memetic communities share these underlying principles expressed by Tönnies as those aspects of the community affect the presentation and messaging of memetic content. Reddit communities, for example, often codify those effects in the rules for posting content on subreddits (Crossman, 2020).

Urban centers contained the **Gesellschaft** spirit within their borders. Gesellschaft explains the modern, industrial experience as primarily consisting of indirect interactions among people living in the same city. The by-product of those interactions is that citizens have this level of disconnection with others. Most daily actions are handled via impersonal (read as "non-face-to-face") transactions with people that have indirect and weak social ties. There is a rational driving force that maintains the social order within the collective. Memes also play a role in this form of society. Daily life within this environment is marked with characteristics that meme creators living there can quickly turn into memetic content. The United States Postal Service's speed is one such example, with memes featuring Newman from Seinfeld, turtles delivering the mails, and other representations of this service that resonate with citizens.

Like other theoretical models, Gemeinschaft and Gesellschaft have no perfect examples in the real world. Most places where people live, work, play, and interact with one another will have aspects of both. Tönnies' models explain the way that social orders work in cities and towns. The bureaucratic components of daily life are the Gesellschaft, as are the policies that drive government action. The feeling that you belong to a city or your hometown is Gemeinschaft, as are the common characteristics you share with your high school classmates. People who live in Chicago experience Gemeinschaft when they talk about their favorite pizza place, their favorite sports team[14], or the city flag (Mars, 2015). Gesellschaft is experienced in paying a water bill at your village hall or attending a village council meeting.

---

[14]I was going to add "Daaaaa Bears!" reference, but figured it was too old.

Memetic communities develop not because all members talk using memetic communication or even mimic each other's actions. It would be fair to argue that it would be more (to borrow the Star Trek allegories previously used) Borgian in nature as the community would be a hivemind instead of allowing community members to express themselves freely. Communities are memetic in nature when they use the allegorical communication model to develop quasi-personal relationships on the social media service (Gemeinschaft) through the limitations of the user interface that controls the interactions that social network members can have (Gesellschaft). Memes express the spirit of the given community (Gemeinschaft) by crafting memetic content with a graphic design program, a classic Gesellschaft tool.

THE THERAPEUTIC CONSIDERATION

It should be no surprise that the therapeutic considerations based on this chapter are grounded in the realm of social psychology. We addressed aspects of social psychology in the third chapter during the discussion of memetic structures. Communities and collectives are central to this chapter, the third chapter, and the means to work with clients in a therapeutic setting. One of the theses for this book is that people will use memes to find their place in society, connect with others, and gain acceptance for their expression of their beliefs and values. The various case studies, figures, and examples from this book should provide evidence for these claims.

A reasonable therapeutic practice would be having the client pick a meme that they think best represents one of the communities that they spend time online interacting with regularly. The focusing question would be, "what do you think this meme says about that community?" This question works as a point of reflective analysis that might get the client to discuss shared social experiences, beliefs, values, and attitudes that would be more difficult without a prompt of this nature. Following up that previous question could examine why that message or ideology is essential to the community.

Another line of questioning can focus on using repeated symbols and phrases within a collective of memes. "Why is [the visual or phrasing in question] repeatedly used in community memes" allows the client to be the gatekeeper into the community mindset. Their translation of the meaningfulness of those symbols may not be 100% correct due to the "unreliable narrator" aspect of this interaction (Bartesaghi, 2009). However, the client doesn't have to present an accurate representation of the community. Instead, their understanding of community interactions can help the client explain how they think they connect with others online.

The last therapeutic consideration is more in line with an art therapeutic practice. It is fair with this knowledge to have the client create a meme in front of you that they would use to explain to their online community what happened today, during the session, or any other event that the therapist would find significant. A term of art useful in this practice is that the client is "translating in real time" those experiences into content that their community would understand. This "guided ethnography" (Tilton, 2012) becomes the grounding for a conversation of how the client communicates with their community.

Therapists who approach these types of sessions with a social psychological mindset need to be prepared to understand these interactions using an "ethnographic sensibility" to contextualize their interactions (Salmenniemi et al., 2020). Online relationships described by clients might have a parasocial aspect, in so far as the connections have been developed mostly in the client's mind (Daniel, Crawford Jackson, & Westerman, 2018). However, discussing these relationships (parasocial or otherwise) can provide therapists enough information on interacting with their clients.

Works Cited

Ashton, M. C., Lee, K., Perugini, M., Szarota, P., de Vries, R. E., Di Blas, L., Boies, K., & De Raad, B. (2004). A Six-Factor Structure of Personality-Descriptive Adjectives: Solutions From Psycholexical Studies in Seven Languages. *Journal of Personality and Social Psychology, 86*(2), 356-366. doi:10.1037/0022-3514.86.2.356

Bartesaghi, M. (2009). Conversation and psychotherapy: How questioning reveals institutional answers. *Discourse Studies, 11*(2), 153-177.

Bennett, W. L., Freelon, D., & Wells, C. (2010). Changing Citizen Identity and the Rise of a Participatory Media Culture. In L. Sherrod, J. Torney-Purta, & C. Flanagan (Eds.), *Handbook of Research on Civic Engagement in Youth*, 393–423. John Wiley & Sons.

Bourdieu, P. (2021). *The Forms of Capital.* Polity Press.

Burton, J. (2019). Look at Us, We Have Anxiety: Youth, memes, and the power of online cultural politics. *Journal of Childhood Studies, 44*(3), 3-17. doi:10.18357/jcs00019171

Carducci, B. J. (2020). Personality and Consumer Behavior/Lifestyle Analysis. In B. J. Carucci & C. S. Nace (Eds.) *The Wiley Encyclopedia of Personality and Individual Differences: Clinical, Applied, and Cross-Cultural Research*, 581-586. Wiley Publishing.

Crossman, Ashley. (2020, August 27). *Overview of Gemeinschaft and Gesellschaft in Sociology.* Retrieved March 10, 2021 from: https://www.thoughtco.com/gemeinschaft-3026337.

Daniel Jr, E. S., Crawford Jackson, E. C., & Westerman, D. K. (2018). The Influence of Social Media Influencers: Understanding online vaping communities and parasocial interaction through the lens of Taylor's six-segment strategy wheel. *Journal of Interactive Advertising, 18*(2), 96-109.

Duncombe, S. (2002). *Cultural Resistance Reader.* Verso.

Foust , C., & Weathers, C. (2021). Memes in Social Movements 2.0: #JeffCoSchoolBoardHistory and the ouster of conservative education "reforms" in Colorado. In N. Crick (Ed.), *The Rhetoric of Social Movements: Networks, power, and new media*, 135–155. Routledge, Taylor & Francis Group.

Gray, D. E. (2018). *Doing Research in the Real World*. SAGE Publications.

Jurgenson, N. (2011). *Digital Dualism versus Augmented Reality*. Retrieved March 7, 2021 from: https://thesocietypages.org/ cyborgology/2011/02/24/digital-dualism-versus-augmented-reality/.

Leyva, R. (2017). Exploring UK Millennials' Social Media Consumption Patterns and Participation in Elections, Activism, and "Slacktivism". *Social Science Computer Review, 35*(4), 462-479.

Liefbroer, A. C., & Toulemon, L. (2010). Demographic Perspectives on the Transition to Adulthood: An introduction. *Advances in Life Course Research, 15*(2-3), 53-58.

Mars, R. (2015, March). *Why City Flags may be the Worst-designed Thing You've Never Noticed*. Retrieved March 10, 2021 from: https:// www.ted.com/talks/roman_mars_why_city_flags_may_be_the_worst_ designed_thing_you_ve_never_noticed?language=en.

Radovac, L. (2014). Mic Check: Occupy Wall Street and the space of audition. *Communication and Critical/Cultural Studies, 11*(1), 34-41.

Robison, L. J., Shupp, R. S., Jin, S., Siles, M. E., & Ferrarini, T. H. (2012). The Relative Importance of Selfishness and Social Capital Motives. *The Journal of Socio-Economics, 41*(1), 118–127. doi:10.1016/j. socec.2011.10.008

Salmenniemi, S., Bergroth, H., Nurmi, J., & Perheentupa, I. (2020). From Culture to Assemblages. In Assembling Therapeutics: Cultures, Politics and Materiality. 1–20. Routledge.

Siisiäinen, M. (2000). Two Concepts of Social Capital: Bourdieu vs. Putnam. *ISTR Fourth International Conference*. Retrieved March 4, 2021 from: https://www.academia.edu/download/63447495/ Two_Concepts_of_Social_Capital_Bourdieu_vs_Putnam20200527-1180-so4lr1.pdf.

Tilton, S. (2020). *The Journalism Breakdown: Writing multimedia journalism content in an era of changing media systems & economic models*. CFSC Publishing.

Tilton, S. (2012). *First Year Students in a Foreign Fabric: A triangulation study on Facebook as a method of coping/adjustment*. (Doctoral dissertation, Ohio University).

Trauger, A. (2009). Social Agency and Networked Spatial Relations in Sustainable Agriculture. *Area, 41*(2), 117-128.

Wani, R. T. (2019). Socioeconomic Status Scales-modified Kuppuswamy and Udai Pareekh's scale updated for 2019. *Journal of Family Medicine and Primary Care, 8*(6), 1846-1849.

Zhang, M., & Dholakia, N. (2018). Conceptual Framing of Virtuality and Virtual Consumption Research. *Journal of Global Scholars of Marketing Science, 28*(4), 305-319.

CHAPTER 10: MEMES AS A THERAPEUTIC ACT

One of the underlying themes that has propelled the flow of this book is that memes can form a productive part of a therapeutic session with a client due to their ability to help a therapist understand what a client is thinking, how they view the world, or even how they represent a community that the client belongs to. Therapists who support this argument can use memes to address the critical concerns of the client and reframe those concerns by using memetic communication. But the extension of this argument is that the creation and transmission of a meme can be a therapeutic act.

Such an act cannot replace the role of a certified and trained therapist in the process of improving the mental health of a client. Therapy should only be done by a credentialed professional in the mental health field who has done up-to-date research in the various techniques of their profession. Those credentialed professionals must also regularly work with clients to judge how these techniques can be best applied to their general practice. Anything less is malpractice .

This chapter is designed to provide therapists and other mental health practitioners the research and tools to think critically about memes as a mode of communication, a form of social interaction, a collaborative performance, and a status of psychological health. These points focus on statements that the therapist can use to further a dialogue between themselves and their client. Talking about memes as a therapeutic act means defining what a therapeutic act is in this context, how those acts fit within the field of psychology, and how therapists can rationalize the implementation of memetic communication within therapeutic sessions.

DEFINING A THERAPEUTIC ACT

One of the struggles in writing this book was developing an operational definition for therapy. The nature of therapeutic practices has some level of customization, depending on the client's mindset, relationship with their therapist, and the forum where the two interact. Such variations of praxis allow for flexibility in how treatments and sessions are conducted. The beauty of such a nebulous term is that improving one's mental health can address the multitude of issues through a toolbox of therapeutic practices, engaged interactions, and self-reflective exercises. It is with this paradigm of therapy that we can shape an operational definition of a therapeutic act.

Rina Lazar (2000) marks therapeutic acts with the concept of **presentness**, as a means to ground the therapy with the therapist's awareness of how their actions will impact a session with their client. Presentness balances interpreting the client's activities, being mindful in their interactions with the client, and understanding what is happening in the client's mind during the performance of a given set of actions. A detailed analysis of psychoanalytic practices shows a gradual therapeutic shift over the course of decades from asymmetrical activities between the client and the therapist to develop better mental health practices to a symmetrical dialogue focusing on treating the client's issues.

We should focus back on those asymmetrical activities for this chapter, as memes represent the application of therapeutic principles outside of a therapy session. Asymmetrical interactions enable the client to craft something that allows them to express themselves in whatever format that the client can use in the pursuit of improving their emotional and mental well-being and the therapist can analyze the actions taken by the client. Therapists can use focused therapy questions and prompts in these activities to address critical concerns during the time that a client is away from a session, thus allowing clients to be more reflective about their approach to such an exercise. It is this line of thinking that helps us see the power of memes as a therapeutic tool.

If therapists build off of the work completed by a client away from the face-to-face, symmetrical session, progress can be made, and the client can see the progress being made in front of them. Let's focus on one example of how this can happen. In this scenario, a client is having trouble dealing with the stress they are experiencing after the death of a family member. The therapist knows that the client makes and shares memes online. Before the end of the session, the therapist can have the client craft a meme highlighting one positive memory that the client had with the family member using a memetic template as a structure for expressing that positive memory. Angela Matthews (2019) references a similar set of techniques as autoethnographic, Sandra L. Bertman (2018) seems to be addressing this type of therapeutic activity as an act of grief therapy, while Niina Keskinen, Marja Kaunonen, & Anna Liisa Aho (2019) uses photographs as the focusing objects to have clients tell stories about the deceased.

The beauty of such practices and activities is that they get to the heart of that operational definition of a therapeutic act. Each asymmetrical exercise can still have the therapist provide clarity on the parameters or expected output of the assignment if the client requests it, or offer a quick analysis if the therapist's schedule allows. But most of the agency is given back to the client to control some aspects of their therapeutic regimen.

It is helpful, with this knowledge, to explore the broader therapeutic considerations that memes can facilitate in a therapy setting. We will frame these therapeutic considerations by referencing back to the definitions of memes that others have crafted in the first chapter.

THE THERAPEUTIC NATURE OF CULTURAL COMMUNICATION

Most cultural communication is built on using recognizable media narratives so that the crafter of the message (in our examples, this would be the meme creator) can use an economy of content to express a complicated experience or social issue. For example, Workers' Rights can be a complex policy issue that requires nuanced communication to get the point across. But a meme showing Spongebob at the Krusty Krab challenging Mr. Krabs' management style, using Workers' Rights language, can have the same impact.

To talk about the therapeutic impact of cultural communication, we can start with a quote from Stephen Colbert from his January 22, 2020 interview with John Mulaney. Mulaney asked Colbert about "being in the public eye and facing Stephen in the mirror." Colbert's answer gets to the heart of cultural communication.

> I have gotten to a place where I don't want a lot from the audience other than to make them laugh and to make a connection that my internal anxieties, as I express them externally through the joke. When it makes them laugh, I have the sense of camaraderie and community that I'm not crazy to feel this way, because they wouldn't laugh unless they recognized it it in somebody else.

Here Colbert is using the comedy format as the means of making this connection with others. The underlying premise of his quote is that his humor (in the form of a monologue or sketch) is cathartic against his anxiety about current events. This belief also echoes Richard Dawkins's definition of memes as "a unit of cultural transmission." Both Colbert and Dawkins are using cultural references to express shared social experiences that are meaningful to the audience.

This level of cultural communication - being able to express what is happening in the world in a way that resonates with the rest of the community - only occurs if a person is self-reflective enough to understand their relationship with their community and clearly identify its beliefs and values. Effective memetic communication happens when the meme creator is mindful of how their actions impact the rest of their community. Part of this mindfulness comes from the ability of meme creators to tell stories about their experiences and community.

THE THERAPEUTIC NATURE OF TELLING STORIES

Another way to observe mindfulness in a therapeutic session is by allowing a client to tell stories about their experiences. Those stories give the client the ability to explain their stress, anxiety, and other issues worth discussing in the therapeutic setting. Stefan Hammel (2018) addresses the potential and power of using stories in therapeutic sessions in his book *Handbook of Therapeutic Storytelling: Stories and Metaphors in Psychotherapy, Child and Family Therapy, Medical Treatment, Coaching and Supervision*. Hammel writes about the spiritual, pedagogical, and social psychological roles that storytelling can play in deal with health issues.

Beyond the health considerations of helping to reduce the level of discomfort and pain in a hypnotherapy setting, addressing issues associated with addiction in group counseling, or even training medical professionals how to treat patient's ailments, therapeutic storytelling gives the client agency of how to explain what is affecting them and some of the underlying factors that they themselves may not be aware are affecting them. The television show House can provide a mental model of how a client can expose those underlying factors.

For those not familiar with the show House, Gregory House is a fictional character who is the Head of Diagnostic Medicine at the Princeton-Plainsboro Teaching Hospital. An overly simplified (and kinder) way of explaining House's process is that he listens to stories and gets an epiphany when his patient says that magical phrase that triggers the part of House's brain that solves all problems. According to Jerold J. Abrams (2009), there is a level of abductive reasoning that leads House to those conclusions. Both House's process and therapeutic storytelling are built on abductive reasoning to find a solution.

There is some **surprising anomaly** that affects both House's patients and a client practicing therapeutic storytelling. House is presented with a patient with a weird set of ailments, while a therapist might simply have a client with an issue that they wish to address that previous therapies have not been able to treat. Both House and the therapist will listen to their client or patient, interact with them doing various exercises, look over their notes, and discover a pattern in those interactions and notes that generally causes that surprising anomaly **as a matter of course**. Finally, House and the therapist try to **discover what is causing that pattern** to treat or break the connection between the pattern and the client/patient and heal them. Abductive reasoning is a reasonable diagnostic method in the development of a series of therapeutic sessions where memes play a role in those sessions.

A client might show several memes with the same slogans or visuals that can present a pattern that the therapist can then discuss and address. The tangent benefit of seeing these patterns is that the therapist can have the client create a meme that expresses what they think about that pattern or theme among the memes they brought into the session. The client can then verbalize their process and thoughts related to those memes. Developing this verbalization of pattern hits on the client's ability to craft meaningful narratives from describing those patterns to a therapist.

THE THERAPEUTIC NATURE OF FINDING MEANINGFUL NARRATIVES

The only way that these pattern verbalizations help treat a client is if a therapist recognizes what is significant about those patterns. A tool like the *Diagnostic and Statistical Manual of Mental Disorders (DSM-5) or the International Classification of Diseases (ICD)* explains how those disorders present themselves by incorporating diagnostic definitions into those disorders. Diagnostic definitions are clinical connotative classifications of those issues that professionals use to describe those ailments. Since clients traditionally have limited to no access to the *DSM-5* or the *ICD*, they use the layman's tool of focusing on those patterns when recounting problems to a mental professional. Often, the best means of recounting those problems is when the client tells a story about their issues.

The most compelling stories that a client can tell often come out when they are describing how those patterns are meaningful. An old piece of wisdom that explains this meaningfulness comes from the saying, "when we don't know our own history, we create our own mythologies." This saying expresses the need to find meaning in our lives. If we do not understand the root causes of those issues that affect our mental health, we craft a narrative that fits the evidence that we see. If we do not talk to mental health professionals about those issues, that description of society and our community becomes part of who we are. We craft this fictional representation of our world.

Everybody hates us because we are different.

We don't fit it because we will not confirm.

These are the kinds of narratives that we might develop to frame our existence if we do not have the support from professionals. These narratives become visible in the work that we do, namely in crafting memes for those that are able to do this creative work or using memes as part of regular online interactions.

Memes expose these meaningful narratives in a way that few therapeutic techniques can. First, this format allows the client to communicate in a manner they are most comfortable with. Memetic communication, like art and music therapy, allows the client to craft an artifact that gives them the opportunity to bring "unconscious feelings to a conscious level and thereafter exploring them" (BAAT Standing Committee of Arts Therapies Professions, 1989, 5). Memes act as a canvas for expressing beliefs, values, opinions, observations, attitudes, and behaviors that those comfortable with the format. Follow-up questions by the therapist about the meme can present a chance for the meme creator to clarify the narrative they are telling within the memetic artifact.

Meaningfulness and mindfulness are two separate parts of this diagnostic equation as they get to the heart of the client's issues. The meaningfulness of any narrative means that the story hits on the aspects of the storyteller and the audience's beliefs, values, and attitudes that they concern to be important. Suppose the storyteller and the audience both believe that community members must have a high school level of education to engage with the rest of the community. In that case, a meaningful narrative will highlight the importance of learning. Memes that embed the standards of an informed public would be more likely to be shared in those communities compared to those memes that champion stupidity.

Mindfulness about the narrative allows the storyteller and the audience to reflect on why those beliefs, values, and attitudes are essential as part of how people connect with one another. If we extend the previous example, a meaningful meme about education promotes an active learning mindset, in which the end goal is to learn something new every day. A mindful meme would highlight the concept that education means we know more about the world and how to relate to one another. The complexity of memetic communication could use the textual (using a quote by Anthony Bourdain promoting learning about one another), visual (a picture of Anthony Bourdain looking thoughtful), cultural (using what Anthony Bourdain represents as an authentic, thoughtful presenter of world culture), and compositional (typing out the Bourdain quote in Impact font face and placing the words in front of the image of Bourdain) layers of the memes to highlight different aspects of the mindful narrative while reinforcing the central message that being educated means understanding the world and the people living in it (Tilton, 2021).

It's important to remember that most memes depend on others to imitate the style and content within the artifact so that community members can share them from their perspectives. This level of imitation gets us to the fourth way that clients and mental health professionals can use memes in a therapeutic session.

THE THERAPEUTIC NATURE OF IMITATION

One of the areas worth examining in the context of a therapeutic session is the concept of social learning, otherwise known as imitation. Most of the previous research and literature surrounding social learning in the therapeutic setting focused on working with clients in the autism spectrum, with most of the research directed towards children (Fitzpatrick, 2018). The argument for social learning in therapy comes from the neuroscience scholarship on the idea that building up social development via imitation practices helps the client generate the neural circuitry related to the behavioral scaffolds that aid the standard socialization patterns (DeMayo et al., 2019).

It is fair to question how memetic communication builds up the client's behavioral scaffolds, considering that a therapist or mental health professional must view the art of crafting a meme as being conducted between the meme creator and the technology they use to create the meme. One aspect of the equation not addressed in that understanding of memetic content is that the meme creator gets feedback from the community in the form of shares, likes, and comments. Positive feedback of this nature is more likely to encourage the meme creator (and, by extension, those who use the memes) to highlight specific themes and layers within the meme that the community supports or enjoys. We can argue this aspect of highlighting is one of the significant reasons that Spongebob is a metameme.

There is value in giving positive reinforcement based on the client creating memes that build up those behavioral scaffolds to help the person socialize and develop traits that will allow them to feel that they are part of a community outside of their online interactions. The paradox of using digital assets to establish analog interactions is resolved by understanding that these digital assets can help the client imitate real world interactions. Memetic communication is no different from other forms of communication since it allows the communicator to develop the skills to interact with others. Therapists can offer suggestions regarding how to apply memetic communication to real world situations during a consultation.

Understanding memes as a practice of imitation is vital for therapists to acknowledge as there are strong arguments that memes can repeat toxic stereotypes and harmful behaviors. The previous chapters of this book pointed to the harms that come from specific communities (like incels, white supremacists, and hate groups) echoing ideologies via memetic communication. Therapists are more likely to see those ideologies expressed via memetic content (as it relates to art therapies) as opposed to traditional interactions with a client (Hamrick & Byma, 2017; Turner, 2018; Eastwood, 2020). The free level of creative control a meme creator has in their work will provide those critical insights toward their beliefs and values in a manner that would be difficult to achieve through other forms of therapy.

Let's explore how a therapist might gain those insights during a session. One of the Coronavirus pandemic trends is an increase in hate crimes towards Asian-Americans in the United States (Gover, Harper, & Langton, 2020). If a client tends to post or share memes that express anti-Asian sentiments or that promote hate, the therapist will absolutely need to address how the client formed those beliefs. More often than not, a client will not respond to direct questions about this. A therapist is looking for a pattern of content buried in those memetic layers to determine a trendline of hate within the memetic artifacts. Recognizing symbols used by hate groups is helpful in this scenario. Some resources that therapists can use are:

- the Southern Law Poverty Center's "Year in Hate and Extremism" report,

- the Department of Justice›s Hate Crimes website, and

- any reports from the Human Factors/Behavioral Sciences Division of the Department of Homeland Security›s Science & Technology Directorate.

Using those resources as the foundation for framing questions might help the therapist address the language of hate that pops up in memetic communication. The best wisdom when it comes to intervening with a client about this type of language is by working with colleagues that have experience in treating clients who have exhibited this type of behavior in the past and what actions that took in alleviating such behaviors. Seeing the praxis of others plus using national resources can help begin a dialogue to help clients with this level of pain.

THE THERAPEUTIC NATURE OF EXPRESSING ONE'S SELF

People are more comfortable using hate symbols, stereotypes, and racially aggressive language in memes because people feel a level of disconnection between themselves and other people due to the lack of direct interactions. Partly this is due to the quasi-anonymous nature of online communication. Most people use a profile name as their primary form of identification online. This separation of online expressions from a person's real world behaviors and interactions allows that person to present "pieces of themselves" on online communities beyond the "performances" one would give when connecting with others in real world spaces (Goffman, 2008).

It is important to note when discussing a profile name being a quasi-anonymous representation of a person that services like Facebook that use "real name identifiers" still have a problem with spreading hate via their networks (Ciftci et al., 2017; Leonard et al., 2018; Mondal et al., 2018). The rationale for this problem is that while anonymous interactions fuel anti-social behaviors online, people who are comfortable expressing attitudes in the real world that show contempt for a class, race, gender, sexual orientation, or social status will be more expressive of those positions online. In turn, they will find groups that support those attitudes and refine them to become that person's beliefs and values. Identifying beliefs and values that can potentially cause harm towards others can be tricky for a therapist. However, these online markers can point to attitudes and opinions grounded in harmful beliefs and values.

Online markers (like memes) act as a proxy for political communication online, which people will avoid talking about face-to-face (Barnidge et al., 2019). Mainly, scholars can point to the need to express oneself outweighing the consideration of how those interactions will impact others as a primary reason for this increased exposure regardless of whether the person can be directly identified as the one expressing those opinions (Wu & Atkins, 2018). A by-product of this type of expression is a narrative flattening of the underlying supporting elements of a given topic or issue (Tilton, 2020).

Narrative flattening refers to simplifying a complex story into two or three bullet points that others can easily share. An example of such a narrative flattening occurred at the time of writing this book. The ship "Ever Given" blocking the Suez Canal became a platform for everything, including trolling the first female Egyptian ship captain (even though she was more than 200 miles away from the Ever Given at the time of the blockage), showing how we are dealing with the stress of the pandemic (using the photo of the little excavator trying to dig the ship free), or rejecting the modern world. The underlying narrative is much more complex than a general audience would typically understand (Raghavan, O'Grady, & Hendrix, 2021) and makes expressing one's self that much more difficult.

Understanding the narratives of the topic or issue allows a person to express themselves therapeutically if they are mindful of how the topic or issue impacts them. The central focusing question that a client will need to answer when addressing a subject is "how does this subject truly impact me?" Sometimes we find that our responses to a given subject are merely echoes of points coming from our communities and media sources we choose. The problem that arises from that simple echoing is that the world is more complicated than a single slogan or talking point. Memes can express the complexity of a subject if the meme creator can identify the significance of the subject. The meme creator must also explain why the community should care about the subject through an ethical and moral presentation about the connection between the subject and the community. Most of the time, a meme does not treat the matter with the thoughtfulness it deserves. A therapist must understand how the subject impacts their client to address their client's issues.

THE THERAPEUTIC NATURE OF REMIXING CONTENT

Moving away from the more negative aspects of memetic culture and communication, a mental health professional must appreciate the therapeutic power of cutting and pasting together a project using mediated works. Therapists have had clients cut out pictures and headlines from newspapers, magazines, and other printed works to craft a goal, dream, or vision board. These creative works are designed to help people visualize their plans and imagine an ideal home and work life (Burton & Lent, 2016; Waalkes, Gonzalez, & Brunson, 2019; Benedict, 2020). Often these works help the client develop solutions that can move them closer to the desired outcome.

Clients remixing other works from popular culture is therapeutic for a few reasons. The most significant of these reasons is that they have agency over their story. Memetic content allows clients to "cross paths" with the characters that read about, listen to, or watch. A client can feel like they control Deadpool by placing him in a situation that the client is familiar with or telling a story that the client is too self-conscious to share with others—for example, using Deadpool to express the fear of being laughed at, giving a speech in public, or failing at a project. Deadpool, like other superheroes, allows the client to project internal struggles externally (Scarlet, 2018).

To extend this narrative a bit further, we should recognize that remixing content into memes gives the meme creator a way to express their views and reality as a media construction. Media constructions are powerful modes of communication. They use multiple mediums to deliver a meaningful message to an audience. Memes work because our understanding of the world around us is built on giving meaning to what we experience, and that meaning is based on our values. These media constructions make the abstraction of personal values and meanings into the concrete form of a visual encoded in a digital file.

This visual work is the way that a person tells their story of how they see the world. A story changes when additional characters are added, it's presented from a different vantagepoint, the location moves, or the narrator's focus shifts. If we accept the premise (from the first chapter) that a meme tells the story from the creator's viewpoint and that memes are the mediated constructions built on a series of layers, we know that we can start to change that story by adding or taking away layers. Mental health professionals can determine which of those layers are meaningful to the client and, if they are harmful to the client's mental health or social well-being, adjust them as needed.

Remixing content is a calming means to express oneself. The various mediated pieces that a meme creator uses to craft their works give them clarity about the message they are sending to their community. Suppose the community responds with positive feedback to a meme creator's work. In that case, it could create a feedback loop within the community that reinforces the person's position in the group and makes them more willing to share their work in the future.

THE THERAPEUTIC NATURE OF SOCIAL INTERACTIONS

The last therapeutic power of memetic communication is that it helps us socialize in ways that more traditional forms of communication cannot. It can be hard to talk about social inequality, but we can share memes about some relevant talking points. Abstract emotions like love, frustration, or even depression have been difficult for even talented wordsmiths to declare. Still, the right meme can trigger something in our brains that makes that abstract feeling more concrete and tangible to the rest of us. The world is too complex for one single image to express a range of emotions to others. Memes are flexible and complex enough that they allow us new pathways to interact with one another.

Those social interactions created by memes build a shared social experience because, as Calum Marsh (2019) for the National Post pointed out:

> This is to some extent true of all internet memes — because what is an internet meme, really, if not an inside joke whose knowing group extends to an online multitude that shares nothing else in common? Social media is uniquely capable of disseminating jokes and references and of conferring on its users a little of that community feeling, but one that tens of thousands, sometimes millions, can share in the same kind of private language enjoyed by friends on a drastically smaller scale.

Memes amplify those community feelings by providing a guide to what the community is thinking. Are we happy that it is Taco Tuesday? There's a meme for that. Sad about the losing streak of your favorite team? Meme your feelings, and the community will sympathetically respond. Understanding how to craft memes is like being a poet or novelist with a command of language. The difference is that memetic communication requires multiple literacies to be effective.

This amplification of community feelings works outside of online interactions as well. We have become more comfortable talking to others about memes we have seen online to explain what we think about them or how they make us feel. By publicly processing memetic communication, it allows us to discuss topics and issues of community concern, as the memes become a proxy for engaging with the facts and observations that we have about those subjects. People across the political spectrum can address caustic areas of discussion like gun rights, abortion, immigration, or welfare by using the memes as the focal points instead of one another. The visual becomes a nexus of focus, similar to how a professor uses PowerPoint slides when teaching a class. Both divert attention away from the person and towards the inanimate object.

Finally, it is essential to note that memes tend to be fun to share. There is little effort required to create or find the right meme to share. They speak to our emotional and social mindset at the time they were posted. In turn, those memetic artifacts become our public journal of how we were feeling during a given period of our lives. Look over your past postings online. More than likely, you'll find a meme that might not be meaningful or significant now. But it was meaningful or significant at the time you posted the meme.

ADRIAN HILL AND HOW MEMES FIT THE MOLD OF ART THERAPY

It seems apt to wrap the last of the memetic acts with the first person to give a name to the connection of therapeutic practices with the process of artistic creation. The London Art Therapy Centre credits Hill for developing the concept of art therapy in his 1945 book *Art Versus Illness.* He first described a sense of joy when crafting beautiful works to improve the dreary outlook and depressing view one would experience while being in a mental health facility. The value of art therapy increased when he discovered that the images could improve patients' self-confidence and give them the agency to use the medium to explain the issues they are facing in a way that talking might not be able to do.

This technique allows people to heal by first building up the skill sets of the clients. Hill's case taught his clients to feel comfortable doodling to ease them into other artistic techniques and provide guidance along the way. Therapists with basic design skills can help clients develop memes using Hill's teaching practices. Start with the basics first, then move on. Use a meme creator online to create the first set of memes in the clinical setting; then, the client can use graphic design programs at home. In-person sessions can be devoted to playing around with the tool, having the client feel that their work has value in the therapeutic session, and looking over work that the client enjoys. The client's homework is more about applying what they have learned or experienced in the therapy session to memes to show their therapist later.

Memetic content lends itself nicely to art therapy practices. It allows clients to use various mediums to take agency in their treatment by applying their interactions with their therapist to the digital memetic format. Also, therapists that understand memetic content can analyze the work being created by the client and go over essential aspects with the meme. This memetic content becomes additional information that helps the therapist understand the client better.

Hill's work in art therapy centers around the idea that therapists cannot heal clients if they are bored. Keeping the mind active makes it more likely that the clients will not focus on the negative beliefs, values, and behaviors that impact their road to good mental health. Memetic content creation can engage the client in directing their time, energy, and attention exercises that help maintain a sense of order in the client's life.

THREADING THE THERAPEUTIC NEEDLE

In concluding this book, I will discuss how we attempted to thread the needle between three critical concepts. Memes should be thought of as less of a catch-all term for digital content on social media and better understood as a means of expression using complex communication constructions. We should also have a keener understanding of how people use this mode of expression to reveal their beliefs and values to their community. Finally, mental health professionals should be better able to apply the concepts addressed in this book in a therapeutic setting to help clients. Each chapter provided the foundations for using memetic content in therapeutic sessions.

Therapists do not need to be experts in graphic design, Internet culture, or even the meaningful signs within a community. Instead, engaging in the memetic content creation process allows the therapists to communicate with the client using non-traditional methods, hopefully leading to a breakthrough during a session.

Works Cited

Abrams, J.J. (2009). The Logic of Guesswork in Sherlock and House. In William Irwin & Henry Jacoby (Eds.) *House and Philosophy: Everybody lies*. 55-70. John Wiley & Sons.

Barnidge, M., Kim, B., Sherrill, L. A., Luknar, Ž., & Zhang, J. (2019). Perceived Exposure to and Avoidance of Hate Speech in Various Communication Settings. *Telematics and Informatics, 44*, 101263. doi:10.1016/j.tele.2019.101263

Benedict, B. C. (2020). Using Vision Boards to Reflect on Relevant Experiences and Envision Ideal Futures. *College Teaching*, 1-2.

Bertman, S. L. (2018). *Grief and the Healing Arts: Creativity as therapy*. Routledge.

British Association of Art Therapists' Standing Committee of Arts Therapies Professions. (1989). *Artists and Arts Therapies*. Carnegie UK Trust.

Burton, L., & Lent, J. (2016). The Use of Vision Boards as a Therapeutic Intervention. *Journal of Creativity in Mental Health, 11*(1), 52-65.

Ciftci, T., Gashi, L., Hoffmann, R., Bahr, D., Ilhan, A., & Fietkiewicz, K. (2017). Hate Speech on Facebook. In *Proceedings of the 4th European Conference on Social Media, ECSM 2017* (pp. 425-433).

DeMayo, M. M., Young, L. J., Hickie, I. B., Song, Y. J. C., & Guastella, A. J. (2019). Circuits for Social Learning: A unified model and application to Autism Spectrum Disorder. *Neuroscience & Biobehavioral Reviews, 107*, 388-398.

Eastwood, C. (2020). White Privilege and Art Therapy in the UK: Are we doing the work? *International Journal of Art Therapy*, 1-9. doi:10.1080/1 7454832.2020.1856159

Fitzpatrick, M. (2018). Mirroring, Social Learning and Dance Movement Therapy with Childhood Autism Spectrum Disorder: A literature review. *Expressive Therapies Capstone Theses. 20*. Retrieved March 29, 2021 from: https://digitalcommons.lesley.edu/expressive_theses/20.

Goffman, E. (2008). *The Presentation of Self in Everyday Life*. Anchor Books.

Gover, A. R., Harper, S. B., & Langton, L. (2020). Anti-Asian Hate Crime During the COVID-19 Pandemic: Exploring the reproduction of inequality. *American Journal of Criminal Justice, 45*(4), 647-667.

Hammel, S. (2018). *Handbook of Therapeutic Storytelling: Stories and metaphors in psychotherapy, child and family therapy, medical treatment, coaching and supervision.* Routledge.

Hamrick, C., & Byma, C. (2017). Know History, Know Self: Art therapists' responsibility to dismantle white supremacy. *Art Therapy, 34*(3), 106-111.

Hill, A. (1948). *Art Versus Illness: A study of art therapy.* George Allen and Unwin.

Keskinen, N., Kaunonen, M. & Aho, A.L (2019). How Loved Ones Express Grief After the Death of a Child by Sharing Photographs on Facebook. *Journal of Loss and Trauma. 24*(7). 609-624. https://doi.org/1 0.1080/15325024.2019.1586186

Lazar, R. (2000). Presentness: An intersubjective dimension of the therapeutic act. *The American Journal of Psychotherapy. 54*(3). https:// doi.org/10.1176/appi.psychotherapy.2000.54.3.340

Leonhard, L., Rueß, C., Obermaier, M., & Reinemann, C. (2018). Perceiving Threat and Feeling Responsible: How severity of hate speech, number of bystanders, and prior reactions of others affect bystanders' intention to counterargue against hate speech on Facebook. *SCM Studies in Communication and Media, 7*(4), 555-579.

Matthews, A. (2019). Writing through Grief: Using autoethnography to help process grief after the death of a loved one. *Methodological Innovations. 12*(3). doi:10.1177/2059799119889569

Marsh, C. (2019). How Internet Memes and Inside Jokes Create a Private Language that Makes us Feel like we Belong. Retrieved April 15, 2021 from: https://nationalpost.com/entertainment/

how-internet-memes-and-inside-jokes-create-a-private-language-that-makes-us-feel-like-we-belong.

Mondal, M., Silva, L. A., Correa, D., & Benevenuto, F. (2018). Characterizing Usage of Explicit Hate Expressions in Social Media. *New Review of Hypermedia and Multimedia, 24*(2), 110-130.

Raghavan, S., O'Grady, S., & Hendrix, S. (2021). Inside the 144-hour Scramble to Free the Giant Ship Stuck in the Suez Canal. *The Washington Post*. Retrieved April 4, 2021 from: https://www.washingtonpost.com/world/middle_east/suez-canal-ever-given-ship/2021/03/31/8849b85c-9154-11eb-aadc-af78701a30ca_story.html.

Scarlet, J. (2018). *Superhero Therapy: A hero's journey through acceptance and commitment therapy*. Constable & Robinson.

Tilton, S. (2021). A Layover of Food: Understanding Anthony Bourdain's approach of describing cultures through culinary interactions and journalism. In CarrieLynn D. Reinhard, Julia E. Largent, & Bertha Chin (Eds.) *Eating Fandom: Intersections between fans and food cultures*. 89-104. Routledge.

Tilton, S. (2020). *The Journalism Breakdown: Writing mulitmedia journalism content in an era of changing media systems & economic models*. CFSC Publishing.

Turner, D. D. (2018). 'You Shall Not Replace Us!' White supremacy, psychotherapy and decolonisation. *Journal of Critical Psychology, Counselling and Psychotherapy, 18*(1), 1-12.

Waalkes, P. L., Gonzalez, L. M., & Brunson, C. N. (2019). Vision boards and adolescent career counseling: A culturally responsive approach. *Journal of Creativity in Mental Health, 14*(2), 205-216.

Wu, T. Y., & Atkin, D. J. (2018). To Comment or Not to Comment: Examining the influences of anonymity and social support on one's willingness to express in online news discussions. *New Media & Society, 20*(12), 4512-4532.

POSTSCRIPT: THE DEATH AND EVOLUTION OF MEMETIC CONTENT

To wrap up some loose ends, we should go to the end. Specifically, the last class sessions of the Memetic Communication course that was the basis of writing this book. One of the last topics we cover is the "Death of Memes." It is usually a free-form session in which five focusing points are placed on the screen. We discuss each of the statements' merit, and whether it represents a position that the class supports and how we arrived at that statement.

This classroom experience is built on Mike Rugnetta's[15] template for conducting conversations about popular culture and its influence on society during his tenure as host of the PBS Idea Channel on YouTube[16]. Rugnetta is adamant that the audience is "allowed to engage in the ideas that are being expressed," with ideas being defined as "all subjects of mental activity, all things that you think with or about" (2017). These ideas are mental representations of the world that one would not consider "obvious or boring." They would be the ones that people would consider complicated and worth the time, attention, and engagement to discuss thoughtfully. Concepts are those ideas within this discussion that tend to be impactful to an audience and examined over a long period of time.

It is in this spirit that we will begin this postscript. Here's an idea: when memes die, it is like the beach of the Internet being

---

[15]writes smart things, is a smart dude

[16]honestly if you have never seen a single episode, please put down this book and watch one, or two, or a dozen episodes

washed back into the sea of chaos and nothingness. To reach this point, we need to address a few points first.

MEMES ARE THE FOUNDATION OF INTERNET INTERACTIONS

In his book *The World Made Meme*, Ryan Milner (2018) argues that memes are a "lingua franca of online life." **Lingua franca** refers to any common language that allows two or more non-naive speakers to communicate among themselves. Latin, Swahili, and Esperanto have served as a spoken or written lingua franca from time to time. The addition of memes to this linguistic grouping is because memes help express emotions, ideas, and concepts clearly to others if the textual layer is not present and the other layers transcend traditional language barriers. There is another vantage point that addresses this same point in a more impactful way.

Another perspective comes from Romanian philosopher Emil Cioran (2012), who wrote in *Anathemas and Admirations* that "one does not inhabit a country; one inhabits a language. That is our country, our fatherland - and no other." This quote is a perfect way to frame Internet interactions as the borders of countries that fade away into the mass hallucination that is the modern online user experience. The only citizenship requirement of this virtual location is active communication and engagement with others online.

Rugnetta (2015) reinforced this concept during the episode "Is Language a Virus?" and expanded this quote by stating that we feel like we belong together if we share the same language and dialect as a mode of expression. This standard mode of exchanging information and knowledge means that people online can build shared social experiences through communicating those experiences in a common language and referencing those experiences through the shorthand of memetic communication. This exchanging information through Internet interactions acts as the foundation for all communities and cultures online. In short, these actions form the bedrock we all walk on when engaging with others online. We can say that memes act as the bedrock because meme (as a form of language) has a superpower that we often fail to consider.

LANGUAGE CREATES THE REAL FROM THE IMAGINED AND THE ABSTRACT

Nothing exists in the real world until we can name it and/or identify it. This statement does not mean that objects really appear from nothingness or no atoms in things until we acknowledge their existence. Memes have the capability to express emotions and ideas that we didn't know how to communicate. We understand words have had this power for a long time. It is possible that we did not realize that we were more aware of taking care of ourselves during the darkness and cold of the winter by focusing on our well-being until we learned there was a name for that, **hygge**. Also, that "back-of-the-brain" impulse to take joy in the misery of others comes to light when we learn the term **schadenfreude**. Memes even can speak to experiences, ideas, and opinions that we did not know how to codify. That awareness is vital as it gives us the ability to understand the lay of the land.

One of the memetic examples that seem to express a concept that was hard to describe or articulate is the Steve Buscemi "`how do you do, fellow kids" image macro. It is the crystallization of feeling older, out of place in a younger crowd, and trying to overcompensate to fit in. It is such a universal experience that even government organizations can use it effectively.

Figure 21: Example of the New Zealand Parliament feed using the Steve Buscemi "how do you do, fellow kids" image macro as a means of addressing a misunderstanding related to the term "ok, boomer." Source: https://twitter.com/NZParliament/status/1191854658773385216

Explaining the level of awkwardness via a meme is like when a stand-up comedian makes an observation about the real world as a witty set-up of a joke. Comedians take those thoughts and state them creatively. They make the raw abstraction of the human condition into a neatly spoken quip with a punchline. Memes have this same power as they can take the atoms of popular culture content and turn them into an object that speaks in one image, which would take more than a thousand words to say out loud. People use that power to address the complexity of life, the universe, and everything.

People can use memes as there are two essential characteristics at the heart of most memetic content; they are interdisciplinary and intertextual forms of communication. We can argue that it is interdisciplinary as memetic communication often lacks one of the characteristics that defines most other forms of communication; memetic communication is not egocentric, but being aware of oneself and one's relationship to the rest of the community or society. To have that level of awareness means that a person needs to develop a critical mind. Memes can help build that critical mind if a person understands all of the underlying support structure that helps create a meme. If the memetic content creation process one follows merely slaps a funny quote on top of an absurd picture, this creation is more of an artistic work than communication. It is this abstract expression of something that the meme creator themselves may not fully understand. The communication complexity of memes comes from the intertextuality of these works.

EVERYTHING IS IMAGINED TO ME UNTIL I CAN PROVE IT IS REAL

Memes have a natural way of placing both the meme creator and the audience into the same mental place. Part of this is due to the media's ability to be "theater of the mind" since the days of radio. We can be transported to someplace else with a good narrative and descriptive textual imagery that moves the mind from the present now of a current location to anywhere else the content creator crafts. Use the imagery from a travel show to think we are on a beautiful sunny beach even though we are in a cold part of the United States during the darkest part of the long winter season. Memes can temporarily perform this ability by having the audience recall the various pieces of media used in a meme and evoke their experiences when they were initially exposed to those works.

Stephenson (2014) brings up this concept in his novel *Snow Crash*. The novel's central premise is that language acts as a code that can program a response into the mind of the receiver of that information. In his book *The Shape of the Signifier: 1967 to the End of History*, Walter Michaels (2006) argues that Stephenson's view is a simplified view of the "magic bullet" theory of communication. Words get injected into the brain and overwhelm the neural network that forms the basic actions. It is better to argue that memes, like all forms of language, represent a series of meaningful signs that trigger individuals' responses based on their beliefs, values, experiences, and viewpoints of the world. It is also that use of language that approaches the question of how we view reality. Understanding how others approach the reality of their situations was addressed Peter Elbow, an Emeritus Professor of English at the University of Massachusetts Amherst.

Elbow (1998) described in his book *Writing Without Teachers* the concepts of **The Doubting Game** vs. The Believing Game. Playing The Doubting Game means that we frame our view of continuously challenging named theories, claims of expertise, and ideas of reality to test the validity of those theories, claims, and ideas. It's how we deconstruct concepts to make sense of the world. People traditionally imagine this deconstruction is what happens during critical thinking (Rugnetta, 2017). Elbow, Rugnetta, and others have suggested adding to this understanding of critical thinking.

The Believing Game comes from the standpoint that critical thinking should attempt to welcome new theories, claims, and ideas to order how they fit into our understanding of the world. This welcoming stance should not be done to create debatable counterpoints against those concepts; instead, it is done with the intent to put you in the mindset of those that believe those ideas and see the world from their vantagepoint. It is essential to state that The Believing Game does not ask you to take up your mindset to take on this perspective completely. It asks the player to walk a little bit, staring through their eyes to see the world.

Memes tend to play both games depending on the position that the meme creators want to express and how memetic structure members feel about that position. Those memes that take on a more propaganda mode of messaging will use both to make you doubt the social norms and believe that a politician, movement, political party, or organization has the correct answers to solve all of the problems that you see with the world. Ethical use of memes should use The Believing Game to express positions outside the audience's daily experience by knowing the meme creator's reality and The Doubting Game to point out the paradoxes of logic, emotion, and ethos. Both can serve a purpose as long as they are not done to extremes.

MEMES ARE THE LAND AND STRUCTURE OF THE MODERN INTERNET

This middle ground between The Believing Game and The Doubting Game gets us to the fourth focusing point for this postscript. The idea that memes are the land and the structure of the modern Internet experience is related to the concept that memes act as the foundation for cultural expressions and social movements online. They are more than the shared social experiences among members of a community. Bogost's definition of memes is vital to remember as allegorical communication better explains this foundational claim. We can traditionally communicate if we share discrete denotative definitions of the words being used as part of a dialogue. A lack of general meanings would make it difficult, if not impossible, to have meaningful exchanges of information between community members. Memes fit the allegorical communication model better than this denotative model as their interpretation is based on connotative definitions of shared online performances. We remember how to use the "Disaster Girl" meme in Facebook feed with our friends to highlight that we are delighting in the chaos we created, invoke the memetic phrase "Sir, This Is an Arby's" to showoff somebody inappropriate or weird statements, or use the "Is This a Pigeon" meme to spotlight a person's ignorance on Twitter.

Saying the memes act as the land that the modern Internet is built on references communication foundations. To completely extend this metaphor (my apologies to Dr. Eric Rothenbuhler, who has mentioned that I tend to overdo my metaphors when building up an argument), the infrastructure and algorithms that support most modern websites allow users to be grounded in what version of reality the content creators are sharing online. Without them, we would be stuck in the first generation of websites with the glyphs referenced in the preface. Social media networks and other dynamic websites are the strata above this previously described infrastructure of the Internet. They are the connective tissue of the memetic networks. Those websites give us the pathways to engage with one another. Finally, memes are the land that allows conversations and arguments to grow (for both good and bad). Memes tend to direct the most engagement between community members and the general public, whether it is for the performance aspects of it (think Ice Bucket Challenge) or their cultural aspects (think memes used during political campaigns).

The structural arguments related to memes relate to the syntax that memes introduce to any conversation. If a given conversation were exclusively textual online, it would follow that language's grammar, structure, and syntax. Visual content would need to follow the community's practices to be understood (either community members used similar images in the past to express a message or the elements within the visual have meaning to the community). Audio and video content works within a conversation as evidence for a given claim within the conversation (using a CDC video to prove a claim about best handwashing practices, for example). Memes introduce a different type of syntax due to their complex and dense messaging.

Memetic syntax is primarily based on the complexity of the various layers that make up the meme. If the memetic artifact is nothing more than text placed on top of an image, it would not be fundamentally different from any other visual content used for online communication. Beyond there are also compositional, cultural, and contextual considerations within the meme, respondents to the meme will tend to have a wide variety of choices. People can choose to address the textual layer alone. However, suppose an animated gif is used to respond to a previously posted animated gif. In that case, there will most likely be a chain of animated gifs following the first two (a gif war). Members of online communities have this flexibility of expression as online communities reflect the dynamic online culture that is the Internet.

Understanding that memes are part of a dynamic online culture means we can address this postscript's central stasis (as opposed to thesis), which is "can memes die, and if so, how?" The short answer is yes. Memes die when they become nothing more than another piece of digital content online or that the mediated work is part of the graffiti that make up the Internet graveyard. The how of their death will take a little bit longer to address.

MEMES THAT ARE NO LONGER RELEVANT

A given meme's death happens when its layers lose their significance and are no longer meaningful in that form. The conceptual layers become disconnected when the meme creator's messaging within the meme is lost or is no longer important. Text can lose its power when the words that at one point might have been novel and interesting become part of the noise (think about the Budweiser "Wassup" advertisements being repeating to absurdity). Overused visuals no longer strike the interest of the viewer. Cultural references lose their meaning as those shows and characters are no longer recognized by the general public (like potentially the previous Budweiser example). Animated gifs might one day be considered annoying relics of a by-gone time, like pop-up ads.

If the definition of memes introduced in the first chapter is a fair representation of memetic content...

> Memes are active, multilayered communication constructions which are influenced by social factors and represent a mode of individual expression, in which meaning-making is controlled by both a community who understands that the whole of the work is greater than the sum of its parts and a collective that places that creative content into some part of the broader cultural industry embedded in society.

...then the death of a given meme is more than those layers losing their significance. The community slowly stops using that meme in favor of other modes of expression. That also means that the meaning within the community also becomes less understood by the general public. Part of the meaning-making happens when the community actively uses the form in a given context. When people stop using the meme, the general public loses the frame of reference of how the work can be used as part of interactions online. The less it is actively used, the less contextual meaning is associated with the meme. Contextual meaning is one of the significant reasons Gestalt theory works to explain a meme's effectiveness. The result of this chain reaction is that a meme dies because all of those definitional points fail slowly, returning the file to another piece of online content.

The erasure of memetic culture is slow, like seawater stealing more of the land and returning it to the ocean. Think about the first set of memetic glyphs referenced in the preface. They would have some significance to those alive in the 1990s and using the Internet. To everybody else, they are artifacts of the past. We no longer use those animated works to entertain us. High-speed Internet has made streaming audio, embedded videos, and video games the default forms of entertainment online.

Just because these more contemporary forms of online entertainment have displaced the past's animated GIFs does not mean that those older memes have entirely disappeared. Instead, dead memes still float in this sea of online content like driftwood. We see them in past interactions on long, forgotten threads in a way that gave them a purpose when they were all shiny and new. Snapshots of our favorite television shows or movies with just the right phrase of text to indicate the mood we were feeling at a given moment.

These legacy reminders in memes on social media feeds, archive websites, and stickers on laptops act as the visual representation of a community or collective's cultural and social history. Those stickers, like what those memes represent, fade over time. This act of entropy is the death of memes. If that were the end of the story, it would be a great place to stop. However, the Internet is a dynamic location where everything evolves.

MEMES ARE REBORN

Memes are reborn and evolve when new communities discover a use for them. Much like many sensational graphic novel series, television shows, or movie franchises, things don't necessarily stay dead in the world of memes. The old and decaying memes find new life when new communities find an appropriate use for them. A simple example that proves this resurrection would be the tale of Pepe the Frog. Pepe the Frog was part of Matt Furie's "Boy's Club" series of comics. Once a symbol of the slacker mindset in the mid-2000s, Pepe became a celebrated icon by alt-right groups:

1. as a means of "celebrating mass shootings," who created "offensive Nazi variations,

2. which were quickly adopted by actual Nazis," and lead to the development of a "Trump-themed Pepe" which was "retweeted by Trump himself,

3. boosting the candidate's support among some of the worst people on the web" (Robertson, 2020).

Furie posted an image of Pepe's funeral to kill him off in an attempt to remove some of the cultural baggage associated with Pepe.

To be reborn, a meme needs to remove as many layers as possible to approach being a blank canvas for the new community or collective to work with. The new memetic structure should have little to no associations with the previous context of the meme, as those associations will hinder the meme's ability to be reborn. If the Hong Kong protestors were involved with alt-right groups in the United States, the Hong Kong protestors would merely be co-oping the ideologies associated with the alt-right usage of Pepe and adopting it as a symbol for a similar purpose. Hong Kong Pepe instead was reborn as a symbol of being free against oppression.

Hong Kong Pepe shows the next step in this process. Memes evolve after being reborn when they can expand beyond being a reconceptualization of a past meme. The alt-right Pepe was primarily a digital symbol when seen on a social media feed akin to "finding a KKK hood in the back of someone's closet" (Ellis, 2019, para 1). In Hong Kong, Pepe was an analog marker that was spray-painted on the side of buildings, found on the laptop of pro-democracy bloggers, and presented as an emergency responder or journalist on the clothing and gear of those protestors. It evolved that those protestors found Pepe "as sinister as Hello Kitty." (para 2). This evolution happens because symbols like Pepe go through a contextual collapse, as the previous cultural capital is lost due to the fluidity of those symbols being shared and remixed on a wide variety of social media outlets (Azar, 2021).

Fluidity is also how past-famous memetic figures find new audiences online. A practical example that shows this fluidity would be how the ESPN docu-series "The Last Dance" reintroduced Michael Jordan to memetic audiences. Jordan was well known for the "Crying Jordan" meme, a "Photoshop meme" that memetic creators add Jordan to various photographic situations. For example, it would not be unusual to see Michael Jordan's face on a mock-up of the Michael Jackson's Thriller album cover, superimposed on top of the Arizona Cardinals football coach, or even Tom Brady's courtroom sketch. "The Last Dance" added to the lexicon of Jordan memes by reusing Jordan's laughter or the quote "...and I took that personally" as a reaction to a situation. Jordan's public persona was not reborn as a meme (as he had a memetic presence in the past); instead, his definition as a memetic figure was reborn (Rosenblatt, 2020).

He became a metameme.

272

Memes that are reborn and evolve will trend towards a meta-meme even if those memes' cultural and contextual meanings are dramatically different. We identify evolved memes as being part of the lexicon of memetic communication. Their metameme status adds to their fluidity. Spongebob + image + text is a meme. Same with Jordan and Pepe. They are the symbols of memetic and digital culture that act as guideposts to allow those in the real world to identify people who understand the significance of those symbols and connect with them offline.

QUO VADIMUS ("WHERE ARE WE GOING?")

Those eagle-eyed readers will note that this book used twenty functional themes to describe memes. They are:

1. Communicative Acts,

2. Performative Acts,

3. Sociological Acts,

4. Psychological Acts,

5. Therapeutic Acts,

6. Cultural Transmitters,

7. Allegorical Communication,

8. Transmitters of Meaningful Information,

9. Imitation of Reality,

10. A Part of Remix Culture,

11. State of Social Interaction,

12. Multilayered Mediated Marks on the World,

273

13. Interpersonal/relational Communication,

14. Demographic Markers,

15. Psychographic Markers,

16. Shared Social Experiences,

17. A Form of Social Agency,

18. A Form of Social Capital,

19. Guideposts for Social Movements, &

20. The Extension of the Social Network.

The same readers might argue that those functional themes do not simplify memes' definition but make it more complicated. Readers would be correct in their assessment of the term. *Meme Life* had essentially three purposes for being written. Psychological professionals could use this book to understand how memes could be used as part of therapeutic practice. The "Therapeutic Consideration" at the end of the first six chapters, along with the description of the various memetic acts in chapters seven through ten, was in service of fulfilling that first purpose. Students of digital and memetic culture could use this book to assess memetic artifacts for more significant scholarly discussion. The first six chapters, along with the theoretical perspectives at the end of each of the chapters, should assist that dialogue. The third purpose is a little more complicated, thus the need for some complexity in those definitions.

It would be logical to assume that this book's more fundamental purpose would be to add to the current meme literature with some insight that a decade of study would provide. That purpose would be more brutal to define as memetic culture's nature has made that pursuit much more complex over the past ten years. This statement goes beyond how memes help entrench people into their ideological and political positions on social media. Meme warfare was explicitly left out of this book as I didn't feel I could connect it effectively to the first two purposes. Others have also done a much more masterful job covering the topic (see Zannettou et al., 2018; Waller, 2017; Prosser, 2006; and Thomas, 2015).

After taking part in this scholarship for nearly a decade, I decided that this book's third purpose was to explore the psychological and sociological significance of meaningful memetic communication on social networks based on memes' social and cultural impact. That purpose was slightly inspired by the diverse body of literature that formed this course's original teaching. The other factor in that decision was actually teaching the class and having thoughtful discussions about the topic with my students, which is why they were name-checked at the beginning of this book.

After reading this book, it is fair to wonder why we are concluding with this reflective analysis of purpose. Mainly, it is an assessment of that third stated purpose. If throughout the book, the reader can articulate some statements about the psychological and sociological significance of meaningful memetic communication on social networks based on memes' social and cultural impact based on not only this book but applying the wisdom of this book to the current state of memetic communication, then I would be happy to think that I succeed in that third stated purpose. It would be the perfect way to end this postscript.

However, as this postscript is entitled "The Death and Evolution of Memes," let's focus on one final point. The beauty of the Internet (ignoring its toxic elements) is its ability to evolve at a pace not seen in humanity's history. More modern tools of production, software, and communication innovations have shaped this worldwide network. If we accept this premise that memes are the perfect encapsulation of the Internet, an individual meme's death is small, considering how the Internet reshapes itself.

John Perry Barlow has this classic quote "The Internet treats censorship as a malfunction and routes around it." We can look at memes the same way. When one meme dies, the layers and experiences associated with that meme get pushed into a temporary void of nothingness. It is temporary as newer memes will capture the shared social experience of the past memes, and the layers of the meme can be repurposed for newer memes. To paraphrase Barlow...

The Internet treats old memes as bits on the recycling bin and finds something new to do with it.

Works Cited

Azar, T. (2021). *Context Collapse: The fluidity of memes and evolution of social commentary.* Retrieved February 22, 2021, from: https://www. nupoliticalreview.com/2020/06/15/context-collapse-the-fluidity-of-memes-and-evolution-of-social-commentary/

Cioran, E. M. (2012). *Anathemas and Admirations.* Skyhorse Publishing.

Elbow, P. (1998). *Writing Without Teachers.* Oxford University Press.

Ellis, E.G. (2019). *Pepe the Frog Means Something Different in Hong Kong—Right?* Retrieved February 22, 2021, from: https://www.wired. com/story/pepe-the-frog-meme-hong-kong/

Felix, G., & Guattari, D. (1987). *A Thousand Plateaus: Capitalism and schizophrenia.* University of Minnesota Press.

Michaels, W. B. (2006). *The Shape of the Signifier: 1967 to the end of history.* Princeton University Press.

Milner, R. M. (2018). *The World Made Meme: Public conversations and participatory media.* Information Society Series.

Robertson, A. (2020). *Pepe the Frog Died, and Part of the Internet Died with Him.* Retrieved February 23, 2021, from: https://www.theverge. com/2020/2/5/21113587/pepe-frog-feels-good-man-matt-furie-trolling-documentary-review-sundance-2020

Rosenblatt, K. (2020). *'The Last Dance' is a Ratings Smash for ESPN. It's also creating an onslaught of Michael Jordan memes.* Retrieved February 23, 2021, from: https://www.nbcnews.com/news/sports/last-dance-ratings-smash-espn-it-s-also-creating-onslaught-n1205626

Rugnetta, M. (2017). *Thinking With Others.* Retrieved February 23, 2021, from: https://www.youtube.com/watch?v=sQ0pny1TA6U

Rugnetta, M. (2015). *Is Language a Virus? Starring Punished "Venom" Snake*. Retrieved February 23, 2021, from: https://www.youtube.com/watch?v=8dNsI3cp6-k

Stephenson, N. (2014). *Snow Crash*. Bragelonne.

BOOK AUTHOR'S BIO

D r. Shane Tilton is an Associate Professor of Multimedia Journalism at the Ohio Northern University. Tilton is also a Fellow for the Ohio Northern University Institute for Civic and Public Policy, the Leyline Geek Therapy Advisory Board, and the Center for Society and Cyberstudies. He was named the 2018 Young Stationers' Prize for his work advancing journalism and communication scholarship and education in United States higher education for nearly two decades. Tilton was honored twice by the Society for Collegiate Journalists as his work advising the Northern Review, the campus newspaper. He was named the 2018 Sheridan Baker Advisor of the Year. Tilton's research normally falls in the realms of collegiate game-based pedagogy, the psychological issues surrounding ludology, multimedia journalism's influence on society, social media engagement, and memetic communication practices. His work on social media and its connection to university life earned him the 2013 Harwood Dissertation Award from the Broadcast Education Association.